FOR CONTINUITY

FOR CONTINUITY

By F. R. LEAVIS

Essay Index Reprint Series

BOOKS FOR LIBRARIES PRESS
FREEPORT, NEW YORK

First Published 1933
Reprinted 1968

LIBRARY OF CONGRESS CATALOG CARD NUMBER:
68-54355

PRINTED IN THE UNITED STATES OF AMERICA

CONTENTS

	PAGE
Prefatory: Marxism and Cultural Continuity	1
Mass Civilisation and Minority Culture	13
"The Literary Mind"	47
What's Wrong with Criticism?	68
Babbitt Buys the World	91
Arnold Bennett: American Version ..	97
John Dos Passos	102
D. H. Lawrence	111
D. H. Lawrence and Professor Irving Babbitt	149
"Under which King, Bezonian?" ..	160
Restatements for Critics	176
"This Poetical Renascence"	190
Joyce and "The Revolution of the Word"	207

PREFATORY: MARXISM AND CULTURAL CONTINUITY

OF the following book the first component piece, *Mass Civilisation and Minority Culture,* appeared as a pamphlet three years ago. If I had rewritten it this year the only change would have been that I should have found for it some more recent illustrations: the reasons for insisting on the case it presents are not less strong now than before. The rest of the book, but for the longer essay on D. H. Lawrence, appeared in *Scrutiny* as articles and reviews, and I do not think it is merely author's vision—parental bias—that makes me see them, reprinted together with the first piece, as forming more than a collection. For they all illustrate, develop and enforce, in ways more and less obvious, the same preoccupation and the same argument—the preoccupation and the argument of *Mass Civilisation and Minority Culture;* and, moreover, misunderstanding possible, it seems, when they were separate will be less easy in the book.

I have not eliminated the repeated mention of *Scrutiny;* that, without a good deal of rewriting, would have been impossible. Indeed, the reminder of the occasional circumstances of production seemed appropriate, since "occasional" in this case intimates not a lack of seriousness and intensity, but the reverse of an academic and purely theoretical spirit, and such a reminder may, for some readers, complement positively the admission, made at the end of this prefatory note, of disabilities on the plane of theoretical exposition.

But perhaps the most common criticism will not be that the preoccupation of the following pages is insufficiently consistent, intense and intent upon practice.

Where something like inconsistency may be fairly charged, and the effects of time found manifest in such ways as to suggest that, here at least, there should have been rewriting rather than reprinting, is in the treatment of D. H. Lawrence. And if I were to rewrite the long essay on him it would certainly be different. But I shall never again, I suppose, be able to give the body of his works the prolonged and intensive frequentation that went to the preparing of that essay, whatever its crudities. It records a serious attempt at stabilising and defining a reaction, and since his, I believe, is pre-eminently a case in which the attitude of those who find him important is likely to be a developing one, and not simple, I feel justified in leaving the reprinted pieces, of changing tone and stress (and it is these chiefly which change), to convey together my sense of Lawrence's significance. At any rate, the procedure is not merely self-indulgence: I cannot read some parts of the early set appraisal without wincing.

About one most important matter I shall certainly (to judge from the latest signs) be told that I am out of date. Discussing, in an article reprinted in this book,[1] the Marxian doctrine of culture, I remarked that it was extremely difficult to determine what precisely orthodoxy was. In the immediate future, I gather from Mr. Edmund Wilson (whom I take to be a good index), the answers to one's questions are going to be different from those of a year ago. Writing on *Art, the Proletariat and Marx* in the *New Republic*[2] for August 23rd of this year, Mr. Wilson tells us that the views that anti-Marxists attribute to Communists are attributed erroneously:

> "It cannot be insisted too strongly . . . that the great Communists have been men who fully understood the importance of art and literature and whose primary idea about them in connection with the revolution was that they wanted to make it possible for more people to get the benefit of them. Nor did they deny the value of the literature and art produced while the bourgeoisie were in the ascendent. On the contrary, they credited to the bourgeoisie the main cultural achievements of the period when the bourgeoisie had been the rising and revolutionary class. They were aware that they themselves derived from the bourgeois culture. And they attacked it only in so far as it was used to defend and cover up the iniquities of the capitalist system."

This is very encouraging. All that we contend for seems to be conceded here. It still, of course, remains to be seen what consensus about these propositions will reveal itself among Communists. Mr. Wilson himself notes that Mr. Granville Hicks

[1] See p. 161 below.

[2] Also in *The Adelphi* for October and November, 1933.

continues to advance hardly consonant ones, and that whereas Engels, "in pointing out how Goethe's work was influenced by his social position, expresses for him high admiration and speaks of him invariably with respect," Mr. Clifton Fadiman, "in the interests presumably of Marxism, is prepared not without impatience to bury Goethe forever." Still, Mr. Wilson is not speaking without book: he refers in his article to his authorities, *Voices of October* and a report on *Art and Literature in Soviet Russia*; and it seems likely that he represents what is to be the common explicit attitude.

But it would be rash to conclude, nevertheless, that we—those of us who, from a view of culture like that attributed by Mr. Wilson to the true Marxist, deduce the need to work very actively for cultural continuity—are going to find Marxists very actively sympathetic. That is not the way, one fears, in which advantage will be taken of the vagueness in which theoretical orthodoxy is still left. "Neither Marx nor his followers," says Mr. Wilson, clearing things up, "believed that there was nothing more in literature and art than the expression of economic appetites; they thought that philosophy and art were part of what Marx called a 'super-structure' which rested on the base of the 'social relations' of the prevailing system of society—social relations which derived their peculiar characteristics from the 'methods of production.' Marx was not a crude mechanist of the kind who used to talk about consciousness as a 'phosphorescence' which ran parallel to, without affecting, physical processes." Marx as a Marxist, one ventures, was not really concerned about literature and art; his concern was for a simplification involving, as an essential condition, the assumption that literature and art would look after themselves. However this may be (and I plead guilty to the familiar charge—I have not minutely studied the Bible), it is certain that for most Marxists the attraction of Marxism is simplicity: it absolves from the duty of wrestling with complexities; above all, the complexities introduced if one agrees that the cultural values—human ends—need more attention than they get in the doctrine, strategy and tactics of the Class War.

What, as a matter of fact, one commonly finds in Marxists is that oblivion of, indifference to, the finer values which is characteristic of a "bourgeois," "capitalist" or Rotarian civilisation—the civilisation produced by a century of the accelerating modern process. Exposing Mr. Granville Hicks's muddle, Mr. Wilson says: "The best American novel about the class struggle I have ever read is Dreiser's *American Tragedy*, which deals with the effects of big bourgeois ideals on a middle-class boy and a country girl: the class struggle is the struggle in the soul of Clyde Griffiths between his desire to get away from his proletarian occupation and up into the world of his rich relatives, and his purely human solidarity with Roberta." The *American Tragedy* may be about class struggle; what it is most remarkable for is the complete unawareness it betrays of any possible ideals other than those of the crude, completely unleavened "bourgeois" world that Dreiser, himself completely of it, exhibits. Mr. Wilson, one does not question it, knows of other values, but it would be difficult to illustrate more aptly than by his comment, which bears no reference to them and could not have been offered if they had been present to his mind, the point made in "*Under Which King, Bezonian?*"[1] regarding the tendency of a preoccupation with the Class War.

Of course the economic maladjustments, inequities and oppressions demand direct attention and demand it urgently, and of course there is a sense in which economic problems are prior. But concentration on them of the kind exemplified by Mr. Wilson works to the consummation of the cultural process of capitalism. What Mr. Wilson forgets in commenting as a Marxist on the *American Tragedy* the world, by the time all the Clydes have been given economic security in which to cultivate their "purely human solidarities" (for comment on this "value" of Dreiser's it is fair to refer to Miss Dudley's book[2] on him), is likely to have forgotten for good.

This fear will, no doubt, be countered with the example of Russia. In Russia Marxism has been rigorously applied, and the result, we are told, is cultural regeneration. Terms as well as facts need evaluating; but it does seem as if the change of attitude registered by Mr. Wilson corresponds to actual developments in Russia. After years of

[1] See p. 172 below. [2] See p. 97 below.

rigorous practice in the spirit of the doctrine preached by Mr. Granville Hicks and his friends, authority in Russia to-day (see, for instance, Mr. Maurice Hindus's *The Great Offensive*) favours the fostering of cultural values that would be recognised as such by one interested in tradition. And practical Marxism in Russia does appear to have released an impressive volume of energy in cultural directions.

All this one can have no desire to ignore or belittle: the world does not offer so much elsewhere for hope to feed upon that one is tempted to reject what is fairly offered by the great Russian experiment. But no sound conclusion can be drawn that does not take account of the ways in which the conditions of the experiment are unique. It is as dangerous to argue from its development as it would be to deduce from the initial revolutionary success the possibility of a repetition elsewhere. Russia is the country in which Trotsky's hope (as summarised by Mr. Wilson) could be: "By the time the people at large had learned to read and write well enough to produce a real culture, the proletariat would have disappeared in the classless socialist society." In such a country, illiterate, inert and economically primitive, a drive for literacy, economic efficiency and social righteousness together might well be expected to bring, along with mechanisation, a cultural awakening.

In England and America conditions are very different: that simple statement hardly needs elaborating. Literacy and mechanisation it is not suggested we need crusade for; and it is certainly not safe to assume that, in these countries, if we concentrate upon social-economic righteousness, the cultural values will assert themselves appropriately in their own good time. They need all the relevant concern of all those who know what they are. But Marxian preoccupations (however enlightened one may be about the relations between culture and the "methods of production") are otherwise directed. And a thousand observers will note with Mr. Wilson the "closing of the literary market to writers who had come out a little too outspokenly on the wrong side of the economic fight" for one capable of insisting that this, after all, doesn't represent the main forms of thwarting and starvation that literary talent and literature suffer to-day.

The reply will come that nevertheless the root-causes are economic. But there is not, explicit or implicit, any tendency here to deny the need—an urgent need—for direct attention to economic and political problems. There are people, says Mr. Wilson, "who, due to an absorption in some special pursuit or study, have the illusion that the intellectual or the aesthetic or the moral activity of man takes place in some sort of vacuum. And there are also people who will admit that literature and art are affected by race, nationality, climate, sexual tendencies and physical constitution, but will not admit that they can be affected by the way in which the author and his readers make their livings or the sources from which they derive their incomes."

The attitude of this book is very different, whether it is literature that is being discussed, or the conditions of literature. It is one that appears to be sanctioned by Mr. Wilson when he says that Marx and Engels were "certainly not proletarians (Engels helped run his father's factory and Marx lived on Engels' money), and they did not attempt to become proletarians. . . . They were aiming at a point of view and a culture beyond those of their bourgeois education; but it was a point of view above classes, not a proletarian point of view—they were trying to develop an intellectual discipline which should lay the foundations for the 'first truly human culture.'"

There *is*, then, a point of view above classes; there *can* be intellectual, aesthetic and moral activity that is not merely an expression of class origin and economic circumstances; there *is* a "human culture" to be aimed at that must be achieved by cultivating a certain autonomy of the human spirit. That the point of view is difficult of attainment makes it the more incumbent on *les clercs* to insist on the possibility and the necessity. The "activity," it is agreed, must be a matter of discipline: one's comment on the Marxian attitude is that, whatever Marx may have intended, it seems positively to discourage the kinds of discipline without which "culture" will indeed be something like a mere function of the economic conditions, of the machinery of civilisation.

The Marxist, in fact (whatever orthodoxy may

be), seems both to under- and to over-rate the possible "autonomy" spoken of above. About the present, and the future thought of as relevant to action, he is toughly sceptical: he admits no reality but the Class War (and the only real differences between classes to-day are economic).[1] About the millennial future, when the classless society shall possess the earth, he is full of the naïvest faith in the capacity of the human spirit for self-direction.

But this is to misrepresent the case: "faith" suggests something far too positive. Actually, in this matter, the (type) Marxist is a good "bourgeois": the essential problem is not present to him, and he shares the incapacity to realise the issues that is characteristic of the civilisation developed under capitalism. It is this incapacity—this "vast and increasing inattention"[2]—that is the enemy in this book; if Marxism figures a good deal as its representative, it is for reasons that may be found not altogether unflattering. The positive preoccupation throughout is, in various ways, with the conditions and function of the extra-individual mind—consciousness, sense of value and memory—that a living culture is; to insist that, in a civilisation of which the machinery becomes more and more overwhelming, the life and authority of this mind must be worked for consciously. The inadequacies and possible mis-suggestions of the term "mind" here are perhaps sufficiently provided for in the pages discussing D. H. Lawrence.

[1] See p. 172 below. [2] See p. 16 below.

That the insistence is not superfluous I am reassured by (among other things) the comments of critics on an article, reprinted in this book, in which I discuss the part of literary criticism in the creation and defining of a "contemporary sensibility."[1] To be so serious about so trivial a matter! To arrive, as the result of earnest thought on the problems of our time, at desiderating (*ridiculus mus*) an authoritative "centre of real consensus," involving such agreement as that "Mr. Eliot and D. H. Lawrence both (however one may 'place' them relatively) demand serious attention, and that the supersession by Book Society standards of the standards that compel this judgment will, if not fiercely and publicly resisted, be a disaster for civilisation"—it is too fatuous, these critics feel, for serious comment.

But for others it will not be so much the intrinsic triviality of the ends in view that provokes derision: even sympathetic critics will ask how they are to be attained. To the questions of the resolute sceptic there is no very impressive answer that can be given. In the context adduced above the suggestion of answer (bearing, there, specifically upon literary criticism) is in no more coercive terms than these: "where there is a steady and responsible practice of criticism a 'centre of real consensus' will, even under present conditions, soon make itself felt." When one passes to the extra-literary implications and refers to education the sceptical questions are as difficult to answer convincingly.

[1] See p. 183 below.

Obviously, in the nature of the case, radical doubt at this point will not be shifted by argument. Whether or not one responds positively to such suggestions as those put forward here depends ultimately upon one's sense of realities; a positive response is a readiness to act as if certain kinds of expectation were reasonable. "Ultimately" in the last sentence is not mere padding: it acknowledges, or rather asserts, the function of critical scrutiny. It may perhaps be retorted that expectations are harboured in this book along with critical findings that make them look not very reasonable. But those who believe in a potential autonomy of human nature such as is implied in the Marxian view of the future should take thought before dismissing as patently futile such initiative and response as are contemplated here—such measure of reliance on intelligence, sanity and humane sense. There is no question (the reminder is not, perhaps, superfluous) of offering an alternative to Marxism—a self-sufficient prescription. The form of the insistence is that, whatever else must be done or attempted (and the simple formula should be suspect), *this* is necessary; and "this" is something that still seems in no danger of being too much attended to. If such modesty and such aims appear ineffective, it might be asked in what ways they are more so than, for instance, incitements to the Class War that are likely to be effective, if at all, in precipitating some Fascist *coup d'état*, with the attendant advance of brutalisation.

MASS CIVILISATION AND MINORITY CULTURE

"And this function is particularly important in our modern world, of which the whole civilisation is, to a much greater degree than the civilisation of Greece and Rome, mechanical and external, and tends constantly to become more so."

Culture and Anarchy. 1869.

FOR Matthew Arnold it was in some ways less difficult. I am not thinking of the so much more desperate plight of culture to-day,[1] but (it is not, at bottom, an unrelated consideration) of the freedom with which he could use such phrases as "the will of God" and "our true selves." To-day one must face problems of definition and formulation where Arnold could pass lightly on. When, for example, having started by saying that culture has always been in minority keeping, I am asked what I mean by "culture," I might (and do) refer the reader to *Culture and Anarchy;* but I know that something more is required.

In any period it is upon a very small minority that the discerning appreciation of art and literature depends: it is (apart from cases of the simple and

[1] "The word, again, which we children of God speak, the voice which most hits our collective thought, the newspaper with the largest circulation in England, nay with the largest circulation in the whole world, is the *Daily Telegraph*!"—*Culture and Anarchy.*

It is the *News of the World* that has the largest circulation to-day.

familiar) only a few who are capable of unprompted, first-hand judgment. They are still a small minority, though a larger one, who are capable of endorsing such first-hand judgment by genuine personal response. The accepted valuations are a kind of paper currency based upon a very small proportion of gold. To the state of such a currency the possibilities of fine living at any time bear a close relation. There is no need to elaborate the metaphor: the nature of the relation is suggested well enough by this passage from Mr. I. A. Richards, which should by now be a *locus classicus :*

> "But it is not true that criticism is a luxury trade. The rearguard of Society cannot be extricated until the vanguard has gone further. Goodwill and intelligence are still too little available. The critic, we have said, is as much concerned with the health of the mind as any doctor with the health of the body. To set up as a critic is to set up as a judge of values. . . . For the arts are inevitably and quite apart from any intentions of the artist an appraisal of existence. Matthew Arnold, when he said that poetry is a criticism of life, was saying something so obvious that it is constantly overlooked. The artist is concerned with the record and perpetuation of the experiences which seem to him most worth having. For reasons which we shall consider . . . he is also the man who is most likely to have experiences of value to record. He is the point at which the growth of the mind shows itself."[1]

This last sentence gives the hint for another metaphor. The minority capable not only of

[1] *The Principles of Literary Criticism,* p. 61.

appreciating Dante, Shakespeare, Donne, Baudelaire, Hardy (to take major instances) but of recognising their latest successors constitute the consciousness of the race (or of a branch of it) at a given time. For such capacity does not belong merely to an isolated aesthetic realm: it implies responsiveness to theory as well as to art, to science and philosophy in so far as these may affect the sense of the human situation and of the nature of life. Upon this minority depends our power of profiting by the finest human experience of the past; they keep alive the subtlest and most perishable parts of tradition. Upon them depend the implicit standards that order the finer living of an age, the sense that this is worth more than that, this rather than that is the direction in which to go, that the centre[1] is here rather than there. In their keeping, to use a metaphor that is metonymy also and will bear a good deal of pondering, is the language, the changing idiom, upon which fine living depends, and without which distinction of spirit is thwarted and incoherent. By "culture" I mean the use of such a language. I do not suppose myself to have produced a tight definition, but the account, I think, will be recognised as adequate by anyone who is likely to read this pamphlet.

It is a commonplace to-day that culture is at a crisis. It is a commonplace more widely accepted

[1] ". . . the mass of the public is without any suspicion that the value of these organs is relative to their being nearer a certain ideal centre of correct information, taste and intelligence, or farther away from it."—*Culture and Anarchy*.

than understood: at any rate, realisation of what the crisis portends does not seem to be common. I am, for instance, sometimes answered that it has all happened before, during the Alexandrian period, or under the Roman Empire. Even if this were true it would hardly be reassuring, and I note the contention mainly in order to record my suspicion that it comes from Spengler,[1] where, of course, authority may also be found for an attitude of proud philosophic indifference. For Spengler, the inexorable cycle moves once more to its inevitable end. But the common absence of concern for what is happening is not to be explained by erudition or philosophy. It is itself a symptom, and a phrase for it comes aptly to hand in Mr. H. G. Wells' new book, *The Autocracy of Mr. Parham*; "Essentially it was a vast and increasing inattention."

It seems, then, not unnecessary to restate the obvious. In support of the belief that the modern phase of human history is unprecedented it is enough to point to the machine. The machine, in the first place, has brought about change in habit and the circumstances of life at a rate for which we have no parallel. The effects of such change may be studied in *Middletown*, a remarkable work of anthropology, dealing (I am afraid it is not superfluous to say) with a typical community of the Middle West. There we see in detail how the automobile (to take one instance) has, in a few years, radically affected

[1] A good account of some aspects of the modern phase may be found in *The Decline of the West*, Vol. II, Ch. IV.

religion,[1] broken up the family, and revolutionised social custom. Change has been so catastrophic that the generations find it hard to adjust themselves to each other, and parents are helpless to deal with their children. It seems unlikely that the conditions of life can be transformed in this way without some injury to the standard of living (to wrest the phrase from the economist): improvisation can hardly replace the delicate traditional adjustments, the mature, inherited codes of habit and valuation, without severe loss, and loss that may be more than temporary. It is a breach in continuity that threatens: what has been inadvertently dropped may be irrecoverable or forgotten.

To this someone will reply that Middletown is America and not England. And it is true that in America change has been more rapid, and its effects have been intensified by the fusion of peoples. But the same processes are at work in England and the western world generally, and at an acceleration. It is a commonplace that we are being Americanised, but again a commonplace that seems, as a rule, to carry little understanding with it. Americanisation is often spoken of as if it were something of which the United States are guilty. But it is something

[1] "One gains a distinct impression that the religious basis of all education was more taken for granted if less talked about thirty-five years ago, when high school 'chapel' was a religio-inspirational service with a 'choir' instead of the 'pep session' which it tends to become to-day." *Middletown*, by R. S. and H. M. Lynd, p. 204. This kind of change, of course, is not due to the automobile alone.

from which Lord Melchett, our "British-speaking"[1] champion, will not save us even if he succeeds in rallying us to meet that American enterprise which he fears, "may cause us to lose a great structure of self-governing brotherhoods whose common existence is of infinite importance to the future continuance of the Anglo-Saxon race, and of the gravest import to the development of all that seems best in our modern civilisation."[2] For those who are most defiant of America do not propose to reverse the processes consequent upon the machine. We are to have greater efficiency, better salesmanship, and more mass-production and standardisation. Now, if the worst effects of mass-production and standardisation were represented by Woolworth's there would be no need to despair. But there are effects that touch the life of the community more seriously. When we consider, for instance, the processes of mass-production and standardisation in the form represented by the Press, it becomes obviously of sinister significance that they should be accompanied by a process of levelling-down.

Of Lord Northcliffe, Mr. Hamilton Fyfe, his admiring biographer, tells us (*Northcliffe: an Intimate Biography*, p. 270):

> "He knew what the mass of newspaper-readers wanted, and he gave it to them. He broke down the dignified idea that the conductors of newspapers

[1] "That would be one of the greatest disasters to the British-speaking people, and one of the greatest disasters to civilisation."—Lord Melchett, *Industry and Politics*, p. 278.

[2] *Ibid.*, p. 281.

should appeal to the intelligent few. He frankly appealed to the unintelligent many. Not in a cynical spirit, not with any feeling of contempt for their tastes; but because on the whole he had more sympathy with them than with the others, and because they were as the sands of the sea in numbers. He did not aim at making opinion less stable, emotion more superficial. He did this, without knowing he did it, because it increased circulation."

Two pages later we are told:

"The Best People did read the *Daily Mail.* It was now seen in first-class railway compartments as much as in third-class. It had made its way from the kitchen and the butler's pantry of the big country house up to the hall table."

"Giving the public what it wants," is, clearly, a modest way of putting it. Lord Northcliffe showed people what they wanted, and showed the Best People that they wanted the same as the rest. It is enough by way of commentary on the phrase to refer to the history of the newspaper press during the last half-century: a history of which the last notable event is the surrender of the *Daily Herald* to the operation of that "psychological Gresham Law" which Mr. Norman Angell notes:

"... the operation of a psychological Gresham Law; just as in commerce debased coin, if there be enough of it, must drive out the sterling, so in the contest of motives, action which corresponds to the more primitive feelings and impulses, to first thoughts and established prejudices, can be stimulated by the modern newspaper far more easily than that prompted by rationalised second thought."[1]

[1] *The Press and the Organisation of Society*, p. 17.

"Let us face the truth," says Mr. Norman Angell further on; "the conditions of the modern Press cause the Bottomleys more and more and the Russells and Dickinsons less and less to form the national character. The forces under review are not merely concerned with the mechanical control of ideas. They transform the national temperament."[1]

All this, again, is commonplace, but commonplace, again, on which it seems necessary to insist. For the same "psychological Gresham Law" has a much wider application than the newspaper press. It applies even more disastrously to the films: more disastrously, because the films have a so much more potent influence.[2] They provide now the main

[1] *Ibid.*, p. 27.

See also p. 19: "When Swift wrote certain of his pamphlets, he presented a point of view contrary to the accepted one, and profoundly affected his country's opinion and policy. Yet at most he circulated a few thousand copies. One of the most important was printed at his own expense. Any printer in a back street could have furnished all the material capital necessary for reaching effectively the whole reading public of the nation. To-day, for an unfamiliar opinion to gain headway against accepted opinion, the mere mechanical equipment of propaganda would be beyond the resources of any ordinary individual."

[2] "The motion picture, by virtue of its intrinsic nature, is a species of amusing and informational Esperanto, and, potentially at least, a species of aesthetic Esperanto of all the arts; if it may be classified as one, the motion picture has in it, perhaps more than any other, the resources of universality. . . . The motion picture tells its stories directly, simply, quickly and elementally, not in words but in pictorial pantomime. To see is not only to believe; it is also in a measure to understand. In theatrical drama, seeing is closely allied with hearing, and hearing, in turn, with mental effort. In the motion picture, seeing is all—or at least nine-tenths of all."—*Encyclopædia Britannica*, 14th Ed.—"Motion Pictures: A Universal Language."

The *Encyclopædia Britannica*, 14th Ed., is itself evidence of what is happening: "humanised, modernised, pictorialised," as the editors announce.

form of recreation in the civilised world; and they involve surrender, under conditions of hypnotic receptivity, to the cheapest emotional appeals, appeals the more insidious because they are associated with a compellingly vivid illusion of actual life. It would be difficult to dispute that the result must be serious damage to the "standard of living" (to use the phrase as before). All this seems so obvious that one is diffident about insisting on it. And yet people will reply by adducing the attempts that have been made to use the film as a serious medium of art. Just as, when broadcasting is in question, they will point out that they have heard good music broadcasted and intelligent lectures. The standardising influence of broadcasting hardly admits of doubt, but since there is here no Hollywood engaged in purely commercial exploitation the levelling-down is not so obvious. But perhaps it will not be disputed that broadcasting, like the films, is in practice mainly a means of passive diversion, and that it tends to make active recreation, especially active use of the mind, more difficult.[1] And such agencies are only

[1] Mr. Edgar Rice Burroughs (creator of Tarzan) in a letter that I have been privileged to see, writes: "It has been discovered through repeated experiments that pictures that require thought for appreciation have invariably been box-office failures. The general public does not wish to think. This fact, probably more than any other, accounts for the success of my stories, for without this specific idea in mind I have, nevertheless, endeavoured to make all of my descriptions so clear that each situation could be visualised readily by any reader precisely as I saw it. My reason for doing this was not based upon a low estimate of general intelligence, but upon the realisation that in improbable situations, such as abound in my work, the greatest pains must be

a beginning. The near future holds rapid developments in store.

Contemplating that deliberate exploitation of the cheap response which characterises our civilisation we may say that a new factor in history is an unprecedented use of applied psychology. This might be thought to flatter Hollywood, but, even so, there can be no room for doubt when we consider advertising, and the progress it has made in two or three decades. (And "advertising" may be taken to cover a great deal more than comes formally under that head.) "It ought to be plain even to the inexperienced," writes an authority, Mr. Gilbert Russell (in *Advertisement Writing*), "that successful copywriting depends upon insight into people's minds: not into individual minds, mark, but into the way average people think and act, and the way they react to suggestions of various kinds." And again: "Advertising is becoming increasingly exact every day. Where instinct used to be enough, it is being replaced by inquiry. Advertising men nowadays don't say, 'The public will buy this article from such and such a motive': they employ what is called market research to find out the buying motives, as exactly as time and money and opportunity permit, from the public itself."

taken to make them appear plausible. I have evolved, therefore, a type of fiction that may be read with the minimum of mental effort." The significance of this for my argument does not need comment. Mr. Burroughs adds that his books sell at over a million copies a year. There is not room here to make the comparisons suggested by such documents as the *Life of James Lackington* (1791).

So, as another authority, Mr. Harold Herd, Principal of the Regent Institute, says (*Bigger Results from Advertising*): "Now that advertising is more and more recruiting the best brains of the country we may look forward to increasingly scientific direction of this great public force."

Mr. Gilbert Russell, who includes in his list of books for "A Copy Writer's Bookshelf" the works of Shakespeare, the Bible, *The Forsyte Saga*, *The Oxford Book of English Verse*, *Fiery Particles* by C. E. Montague and Sir Arthur Quiller-Couch's *The Art of Writing*, tells us that:

> "Competent copy cannot be written except by men who have read lovingly, who have a sense of the romance of words, and of the picturesque and the dramatic phrase; who have versatility enough and judgment enough to know how to write plainly and pungently, or with a certain affectation. Briefly, competent copy is a matter not only of literary skill of a rather high order, but also skill of a particular specialised kind."

The influence of such skill is to be seen in contemporary fiction. For if, as Mr. Thomas Russell (author of "What did you do in the Great War, daddy?"), tells us, "English is the best language in the world for advertising," advertising is doing a great deal for English. It is carrying on the work begun by Mr. Rudyard Kipling, and, where certain important parts of the vocabulary are concerned, making things more difficult for the fastidious. For what is taking place is not something that affects only the environment of culture, stops short, as it were, at the periphery. This should be obvious, but it does not appear to be so to many who would recognise the account I have given above as matter of commonplace. Even those who would agree that there has been an overthrow of standards, that authority has disappeared, and that the currency has been debased and inflated, do not often seem to realise what the catastrophe portends. My aim is to bring this home, if possible, by means of a little concrete evidence. I hope, at any rate, to avert the charge of extravagant pessimism.

For consider, to begin with, Mr. Arnold Bennett. The history of how the author of *The Old Wives' Tale* has since used his creative talents I will not dwell upon further than to suggest that such a history would have been impossible in any other age. It is Mr. Arnold Bennett, the arbiter of taste, that I have chiefly in mind. In this capacity too he has a history. If one reads the articles which he contributed to the *New Age* twenty years ago (they are reprinted in *Books and Authors*) it is to break into admiring comment again and again. It is, for instance, impossible not to applaud when he is impudent about the Professors:

> "I never heard him lecture, but I should imagine that he was an ideal University Extension lecturer. I do not mean this to be in the least complimentary to him as a critic. His book, *Illustrations of Tennyson*, was an entirely sterile exercise, proving on every page that the author had no real perceptions about literature. It simply made creative artists laugh. They knew. His more recent book on modern tendencies

displayed in an acute degree the characteristic inability of the typical professor to toddle alone when released from the leading strings of tradition.

"I fear that most of our professors are in a similar fix. There is Professor George Saintsbury, a regular Albert Memorial of learning."

* * * * *

"It may not be generally known (and I do not state it as a truth) that Professor Raleigh is a distant connection of the celebrated family of Pains, pyrotechnicians."

Yes, it is impossible not to applaud. And yet there is something in the manner—well, twenty years later we find it more pronounced:

"Nevertheless, though performances of Greek plays usually send me to sleep—so far off and incredible is the motivation of them, I murmur about the original author on reading some of the dialogues of Plato: 'This fellow knew exactly how to do it.' And of Homer: 'This fellow knew the whole job.' And of Aristotle: 'This is the only fellow who ever really could do it.' And when I first set eyes on the Acropolis at Athens I said out loud—no mere murmuring: 'These fellows could do it.'" (*Evening Standard*, Jan. 19th, 1928.)

When I try to comment on the manner of this I can only murmur: "Matthew Arnold could have done it." It is, of course, not merely manner: the Man from the North brought something more fundamental with him. There is an ominous note in the first passage I quoted: "It simply made creative artists laugh. They knew." Mr. Bennett is a creative artist, and Mr. Bennett knows. And for some years now Mr. Bennett has been the most powerful maker of literary reputations in England. To compute how many bad books a year, on the average, Mr. Bennett has turned into literature would hardly be worth the labour. It is enough to instance some of his achievements and to quote some of his pontifical utterances from the *Evening Standard*. Here is the typical achievement:

> "Mr. Arnold Bennett's reputation as a maker of 'best sellers' has been heightened by the addition of one more to the list of other people's books which the public has clamoured for on his word.
>
> Last week *Vivandiere* meant nothing to most people, and the name of Miss Phoebe Fenwick Gaye conveyed no more.
>
> Then Mr. Arnold Bennett, in his weekly article on books in the *Evening Standard* mentioned that *Vivandiere* was this young woman's first novel, and that it was very good.
>
> The demand for the book which has suddenly arisen has cleared the first edition right out of existence, and still the clamour goes on. Martin Secker, the publishers, told the *Evening Standard* of the sudden overwhelming demand which followed Mr. Arnold Bennett's praise.
>
> A member of the firm said:
>
> 'The demand was so great that the first edition was completely sold out and we have had to get busy with a second edition, which will be ready to-morrow.'"

Mr. Arnold Bennett made in this way *Jew Süss*. He also made, I understand, *The Bridge of San Luis Rey*; for, though he saw through the academic critics, he takes readily to Academy art. But his critical prowess is best exhibited by quotation from the *Evening Standard*:

Nov. 22nd, 1928.—"*The Golden Age* is a destructive masterpiece."

Dec. 13th, 1928.—"Mr. Eliot is a fine poet—sometimes, if not in that celebrated piece of verse, *The Waste Land*, at the mention of which the very young bow the head in adoration."

May 3rd, 1928.—"Mr. Stanley Baldwin made no mistake about Mary Webb."

Jan. 3rd, 1929.—"The novel is making progress. It has been galvanised by the very important experiments of James Joyce, D. H. Lawrence, R. H. Mottram, and Aldous Huxley: all of whom have brought something new into it. The biggest of these is, or was, James Joyce. . . . R. H. Mottram is a genius. He writes like a genius," etc.

Nov. 8th, 1928.—". . . In particular I have failed to perceive any genuine originality in the method of *Mrs. Dalloway*. If originality there is, it fails of its object of presenting a character. . . . Here is Mr. Muir discussing the modern novel and he makes but passing reference to D. H. Lawrence, and no reference at all to R. H. Mottram, the two novelists who more than any other of their contemporaries continually disclose genuine originality, the two real British geniuses of the new age!"

Jan. 24th, 1929.—" I have just read Edith Sitwell's new poem, *Gold Coast Customs*. In its intense individuality, its frightening freshness of vision, its verbal difficulties, it stands by itself."

Mr. Bennett, we perceive, is a judge of poetry as well as of the novel: he can distinguish. He is adequate to the subtle complexities of Miss Sitwell, but he will stand no nonsense from Mr. Eliot. And he has no misconception about the kind of success that alone can justify a poet:

> "These parasites on society cannot, or apparently will not, understand that the first duty of, for instance, a poet is not to write poetry, but to keep himself in decency, and his wife and children if he has them, to discharge his current obligations, and to provide for old age." (*Evening Standard*, June 9th, 1927.)

No, it was not merely a manner that Mr. Bennett brought with him from the Five Towns. And it is not merely expression that one finds so gross in his critical vocabulary: "Value for money"; "let there be no mistake about it, this is a big book"; "a high class poet"; ". . . I enjoyed reading *Creative Writing*. It is full of chunks of horse-sense about writing." But Mr. Bennett is capable of modesty: it has occurred to him, for instance, to be modest about his qualifications for judging poetry. And his modesty is, if possible, even more damning than his assurance. He writes in *Journal*, 1929:

> "I met a poet there; he was modest; he remarked in a somewhat sad tone that I rarely mentioned poetry in my articles on new books. I told him that I gave poetry a miss for the good reason that I had no technical knowledge of prosody. (True, you can have a knowledge of prosody without having a feeling for poetry, but you cannot properly assess poetry without knowing a lot about prosody.)"

Mr. Bennett will not understand what is meant by saying that this would-be confession is, instead, self-betrayal: so complete is his ignorance about poetry.

How is it that he can go on exposing himself in this way without becoming a by-word and a laughing-stock? (For the author of *The Old Wives' Tale* is a public figure, and differs in this from the minor pontiffs who compete with him in the Sunday papers and elsewhere.) It is that there is no longer an informed and cultivated public. If there is no public to break into a roar of laughter when Mr. Bennett tells us that R. H. Mottram, like James Joyce, is a genius, or that D. H. Lawrence and R. H. Mottram (poor Mr. Mottram!) are the two real British geniuses of the new age, how should there be a public to appreciate Mr. Bennett's modesty about poetry? (For fiction, as we all know, is read and enjoyed.) Why should Mr. Bennett's pontifications make a stir when Mr. J. C. Squire, specialist in poetry and "himself a poet," can, in prefacing one of the best-known anthologies of modern verse (*Selections from Modern Poets*), write:

> "Should our age be remembered by posterity solely as an age during which fifty men had written lyrics of some durability for their truth and beauty, it would not be remembered with contempt. It is in that conviction that I have compiled this anthology";

and Mr. Harold Monro, even more a specialist in poetry and also "himself a poet," in the *Introduction* to *Twentieth Century Poetry*:

> "Is it a great big period, or a minutely small?

> Reply who can? Somebody with whom I was talking cried: 'They are all only poetical persons—*not* poets. Who will be reading them a century hence?' To which I answered: 'There are so many of them that, a century hence, they may appear a kind of Composite Poet; there may be 500 excellent poems proceeding from 100 poets mostly not so great, but well worth remembering a century hence.'"

Such pronouncements could be made only in an age in which there were no standards, no living tradition of poetry spread abroad, and no discriminating public. It is the plight of culture generally that is exemplified here.[1] In the *Advertisement* to the first edition of *Lyrical Ballads* I light on this:

> "An accurate taste in poetry, as in all other arts, Sir Joshua Reynolds has observed, is an acquired talent, which can only be produced by severe thought, and a long continued intercourse with the best models of composition."

When Wordsworth wrote that, severe thought and long-continued intercourse with the best models were more widely possible than now. What distractions have come to beset the life of the mind

[1] "For there is no such gulf between poetry and life as over-literary persons sometimes suppose. There is no gap between our everyday emotional life and the material of poetry. The verbal expression of this life, at its finest, is forced to use the technique of poetry; that is the only essential difference. We cannot avoid the material of poetry. If we do not live in consonance with good poetry, we must live in consonance with bad poetry. And, in fact, the idle hours of most lives are filled with reveries that are simply bad private poetry. On the whole evidence, I do not see how we can avoid the conclusion that a general insensitivity to poetry does witness a low level of general imaginative life."—I. A. RICHARDS, *Practical Criticism*, pp. 319–320.

since then! There seems every reason to believe that the average cultivated person of a century ago was a very much more competent reader than his modern representative. Not only does the modern dissipate himself upon so much more reading of all kinds: the task of acquiring discrimination is much more difficult. A reader who grew up with Wordsworth moved among a limited set of signals (so to speak): the variety was not overwhelming. So he was able to acquire discrimination as he went along. But the modern is exposed to a concourse of signals so bewildering in their variety and number that, unless he is especially gifted or especially favoured, he can hardly begin to discriminate. Here we have the plight of culture in general. The landmarks have shifted, multiplied and crowded upon one another, the distinctions and dividing lines have blurred away, the boundaries are gone, and the arts and literatures of different countries and periods have flowed together, so that, if we revert to the metaphor of "language" for culture, we may, to describe it, adapt the sentence in which Mr. T. S. Eliot describes the intellectual situation: "When there is so much to be known, when there are so many fields of knowledge in which the same words are used with different meanings, when every one knows a little about a great many things, it becomes increasingly difficult for anyone to know whether he knows what he is talking about or not."

We ought not, then, to be surprised that now, when a strong current of criticism is needed as never before, there should hardly be in England a cultivated public large enough to support a serious critical organ. The *Criterion* carries on almost alone. It is accused of being solemn, and seems to owe its new-found security to a specific ecclesiastical interest. For the short-lived *Calendar of Modern Letters*, as intelligent and lively a review as ever appeared in English, died for lack of support. Whatever support the *Dial* may have enjoyed on this side the Atlantic, it now comes no longer, and only the *New Adelphi* is left to carry on with the *Criterion*. There is, of course, the *Times Literary Supplement*, but it would be a misnomer to call it a critical organ. For the hope of intelligent reviewing we are left (apart from the *Criterion* and the *New Adelphi*) to the *Nation and Athenaeum* and the *New Statesman*, and they, of course, have no room for any but short articles.

The critically adult public, then, is very small indeed: they are a very small minority who are capable of fending for themselves amid the smother of new books. But there is a relatively large public that goes for guidance to the *Observer* and the *Sunday Times*, and a still larger one that goes to weeklies like *John o'London's* (which have surprising circulations). Now it would take greater enterprise and vigour than are common in these publics to make much use of the kind of help to be found in such quarters. The reader must have a great deal more done for him. Again we have to learn from America: the problem has been solved there by the Book of the

Month Club and similar organisations. The problem is now rapidly being solved here, where The Book Society has already been followed by The Book Guild.

> "Out of the thousands of books published every year," writes Miss Ethel Manning for the Book Guild, "—there are between 12,000 and 14,000—how on earth is the ordinary person to sift the sheep from the goats? Distinguished critics attempt to guide the public, but they are often so hopelessly 'high brow' and 'precious,' and simply add to the general confusion and bewilderment.
>
> When the aims of The Book Guild were explained to me, therefore, it seemed too good to be true—an organisation which would cater *for the ordinary intelligent reader*, not for the highbrows—an organisation which would realise that *a book can have a good story and a popular appeal and yet be good literature*—be good literature and yet be absorbingly interesting, of the kind you can't put down once you've started, an organisation which would not recommend a book as a work of genius simply because it had been eulogised by some pedantic critic or other, but which would conscientiously sift really good stuff out of the mass of the affected and pretentious which is just as tiresome as the blatantly third rate.
>
> There are so many really good books written nowadays that it is utterly impossible for the ordinary person to keep track of them all—even the critics don't succeed in doing so. The Book Guild by means of its Recommended List of Alternative Titles is able, as it were, to keep its finger on the pulse of the best of contemporary work, whilst at the same time providing something for everybody and that something the best of its kind," etc.

As for the method, we may turn to the official account of "How the Book Society operates":

"Publishers throughout the country are submitting their most important works in advance of publication to the selection committees. From these the Committee select their 'books of the month,' and in addition compile a supplementary list of others they can thoroughly recommend.

"On the morning of publication every member of the Book Society receives a first edition of the book the committee have chosen. Enclosed in this book is a copy of the 'Book Society News' which contains reviews by members of the committee both of the selected book and of those on the supplementary list. If any members feel that the book chosen is not *their* book, they may return it within five days and will receive by return whatever book they select in exchange from the suppplementary list."

Mr. Hugh Walpole, Miss Clemence Dane (author of *Tradition and Hugh Walpole*), Mrs. Sylvia Lynd, Mr. J. B. Priestley (who wrote of a book of Mr. Walpole's: "*Rogue Herries* is a grand tale, a real full-time man's job in fiction, and everybody should read it"), and the President of Magdalen College, Oxford, then, have, with their compeers of The Book Guild, taken into their keeping the future of English taste, and they will undoubtedly have a very great influence.[1] The average member of their

[1] A member is reported as writing: "No man likes to be told what is good for him, it is an affront to his intelligence. Neither will he allow Mr. Walpole nor Mr. Priestley nor John Milton to tell him what to read. But he is simply a fool if he is not impressed by their decisions in matters of literary taste. And that is where the Book Society comes in."

"The speaker had evidently no notion that there was a scale of value for judgments on these topics, and that the judgments

flocks will probably get through a greater amount of respectable reading than before. But the most important way in which their influence will work is suggested by this passage from a book I have already referred to, *Advertisement Writing*, by Mr. Gilbert Russell:

> "Some years ago a manufacturer was making some hundred of different patterns of the same article. His factory was therefore constantly concerned with small runs, necessitating frequent setting-up of machines. This was expensive, and the manufacturing economies of large scale production were out of reach. It was seen that if the number of patterns could be reduced from hundreds to scores, factory economies could be effected. This course was beset with difficulties, however. The retail trade was accustomed to order individual patterns to suit individual shopkeepers, and the travellers were afraid of losing orders if they told their shopkeeper friends that individual preferences and fads could no longer be provided for, and orders must be booked from a score of standard patterns. Nevertheless the manufacturer was determined. What he did was to reduce his hundreds of patterns to the score that were most often ordered. The whole of his marketing policy became one of concentrating selling effort upon this score of patterns. The thing had to be done gradually. But this was the settled purpose which he had in mind, and his advertising policy had to conform to his marketing policy. For instance, in catalogues to the retail trade nearly all the former hundred patterns were mentioned, and most of them illustrated

of the *Saturday Review* ranked high on this scale, and those of the *British Banner* low; the taste of the bathos implanted by nature in the literary judgments of man had never, in my friend's case, encountered any let or hindrance."—*Culture and Anarchy*.

as they had always been, but the score or so of patterns that he was concentrating upon were illustrated in *colour*. And, exactly as expected, the vast bulk of the orders came in for these. Similarly, advertisements emphasised the standard lines, the object of the advertising policy being to educate the public into demanding what the manufacturer wanted to sell, so that the retail trade should order what the public actually demanded. In time, of course, all the patterns were dropped except the standard ones."

This saves a great deal of comment. Standardisation advances to fresh triumphs.

The Book Society has at its command the psychological resources of modern advertising:

"How often, sitting in some strange house, have your eyes wandered to the bookshelves in an effort to get some idea of the character of its owner? The books you read are often a guide to your character. The Book Society will help you to get those books you most want to have on your bookshelf."[1]

We are reminded of the way in which the compatriots of George F. Babbitt are persuaded to express their personalities in "interior decoration." There is, in fact, a strong American flavour about the "literature" of both concerns. Both, for example, make great play with the American adjective "worth-while": "Build a worth-while library!"; "a worth-while book": "I believe that the Book Society will prove to many people that a few pounds spent on new books in the year is a happy and worth-while experience" (Mr. Hugh Walpole). The significance of this use, of course, lies in the atmosphere

[1] *The Books you Read.* Published by the Book Society.

of uplift and hearty mass sentiment that the word brings with it. An appreciative member writes: "Finally, as a member of the Book Society, I am conscious of a pleasant feeling of comradeship, it is something of a great adventure, original, happily conceived, well carried out, with friendly methods of working."—Innocent enough, in all conscience. But there is, belonging to the same vocabulary as "worth-while," another word that the sovereign powers of both organisations use even more—"high-brow." And the attitude behind the word "high-brow" is exhibited with commendable guilelessness by Mr. George A. Birmingham (Canon Hannay) of The Book Guild. This reverend gentleman writes in *The Book Guild Bulletin* for July 14, 1930:

> "The detective novel writers have their own clientele, though they make no appeal to the young ladies who throng the counters of Boots' libraries and but little to the sheep-like crowd who follow the dictates of high-brow literary critics."

Lest the point should be missed he repeats it:

> ". . . not food for the Messrs. Boots' young ladies or for the literary sheep whom I have already mentioned."

If the independent and intelligent critics who unpack the books chosen for them by Mr. George A. Birmingham, Miss Ethel Mannin,[1] Mr. Walpole, and

[1] The *Nation and Athenaeum* reviewer of Miss Mannin's recent book, *Confessions and Impressions*, says: ". . . I confess that the impression her book makes upon me is that it is cheap, crude, vulgar and uneducated."—*Nation and Athenaeum*, August 9, 1930.

Miss Clemence Dane[1] do not know now how they should feel towards the snobs who question the taste of these authorities—then they are not the independent and intelligent critics they are taken for.

"High-brow" is an ominous addition to the English language. I have said earlier that culture has always been in minority keeping. But the minority now is made conscious, not merely of an uncongenial, but of a hostile environment. "Shakespeare," I once heard Mr. Dover Wilson say, "was not a high-brow." True: there were no "high-brows" in Shakespeare's time. It was possible for Shakespeare to write plays that were at once popular drama and poetry that could be appreciated only by an educated minority. *Hamlet* appealed at a number of levels of response, from the highest downwards. The same is true of *Paradise Lost, Clarissa, Tom Jones, Don Juan, The Return of the Native*. The same is not true, Mr. George A. Birmingham might point out, of *The Waste Land, Hugh Selwyn Mauberley, Ulysses* or *To the Lighthouse*. These works are read only by a very small specialised public and are beyond the reach of the vast majority

[1] "And it is easy to believe that the modern English novel, which is suffering so severely nowadays from specialists, high-brows, and cranks, will benefit as thoroughly from its course of Edgar Wallace and Sax Rohmer as it did a century ago from its dose of Monk Lewis, Maturin and Mrs. Radcliffe."—*Tradition and Hugh Walpole*, by Clemence Dane, p. 27.

There is nothing more discussible than this in the windy, pretentious, eloquent vacuity of Miss Dane's book, which received respectful attention on the front page of the *Times Literary Supplement*, July 31, 1930.

of those who consider themselves educated. The age in which the finest creative talent tends to be employed in works of this kind is the age that has given currency to the term "high-brow." But it would be as true to say that the attitude implicit in "high-brow" causes this use of talent as the converse. The minority is being cut off as never before from the powers that rule the world; and as Mr. George A. Birmingham and his friends succeed in refining and standardising and conferring authority upon "the taste of the bathos implanted by nature in the literary judgments of man" (to use Matthew Arnold's phrase), they will make it more and more inevitable that work expressing the finest consciousness of the age should be so specialised as to be accessible only to the minority.

"Civilisation" and "culture" are coming to be antithetical terms. It is not merely that the power and the sense of authority are now divorced from culture, but that some of the most disinterested solicitude for civilisation is apt to be, consciously or unconsciously, inimical to culture. Mr. H. G. Wells, for example, belongs, for the minority, to the past, but it is probable that he represents a good deal of the future. And he returns the compliment paid him by the minority. In his last book, *The Autocracy of Mr. Parham*, he makes his butt, a waxwork grotesque labelled "Oxford Don," representative not only of tribal nationalism, imperialism, and The Old Diplomacy, but also of culture. There is, one gathers, nothing more to be said for art than

Mr. Parham, in the National Gallery, says to Sir Bussy Woodcock. And the book ends with Sir Bussy (representative and defence-mechanism of Mr. Wells) declaring of a proposed newspaper propaganda to Mr. Parham: "It would be up against everything you are." "History is bunk!" said Mr. Henry Ford. Mr. Wells, who is an authority, endorses.

Sir Bussy's is not the only scheme for using a civilised technique on behalf of a civilising education. Dr. John B. Watson (who is vice-president of an advertising concern), writes:[1]

> "We hear of no technique for learning how to behave emotionally or unemotionally. Anybody can teach you to play tennis, drive a motor-car, set type, to paint or to draw. We have schools and instructors for all this, but who has set up a school for teaching us to be afraid and not afraid, to fall in love and to fall out of love, to be jealous or not jealous, to be slow to anger and quick to forget, not to let the sun go down on our wrath, to forgive freely, not to give way to angry passions? And yet some of these modes of behaviour make up the essence of the Christian religion; as a matter of fact, they are part of every civilised code."

So Dr. Watson explains the technique that is to replace the unscientific traditional ways. As for standards of moral and other value, he is modest: he does not dictate:

> "It is not the behaviourist's business to say what is good for society. Society must make up its mind what it wants its members to be and to do; then it

[1] *The Ways of Behaviourism*, p. 48.

is up to the behaviourist to find the methods and technique that will bring the child up in the way it should grow."[1]

He has misgivings, it is true:

"The behaviourist, then, has given society the rough pattern of a new weapon for controlling the individual. Will it use this weapon when perfected as a steam roller to flatten out all that is different in human personalities (which it can do, in spite of 'heredity,' producing thereby a race of conformists)? Or will it use this method wisely?"[2]

But even if Dr. Watson were in charge it would go ill with culture:

"The new things in the universe come from the doers—the chemist, the physicist, the engineer, the biologist, the business man. With them doing leads to thinking, and thinking in turn leads to doing. With the poet, the day-dreamer, thinking leads not to doing but *merely to other words* either spoken or thought; the endless chain of words is never broken."[3]

"We have too many philosophic verbal speculators, rhetoricians, poets and dreamers now."[4]

Dr. Watson, of course, is an American and in England regarded as a crank. But there is reason to suppose that Behaviourism has already had a good deal of practical effect in America. And, in any case, Dr. Watson only exhibits in an extreme form traits commonly to be observed in highly intelligent and disinterested persons of scientific training who devote themselves to the future of humanity. Anyone who has met a Eugenist will recognise these

[1] *The Ways of Behaviourism*, pp. 60–61. [2] *Ibid.*, p. 63.
[3] *Ibid.*, p. 86. [4] *Ibid.*, p. 111.

traits. Major Leonard Darwin, President of the Eugenics Education Society, for instance, thinks that human excellence may, for practical Eugenic purposes, be measured by earning capacity.[1] Then there is Sir Richard Paget, author of the recent important book, *Human Speech*. In a little book called *Babel*, published in the *To-day and To-morrow* series, Sir Richard argues, cogently, that it is time English was deliberately and scientifically improved and standardised as a language of thought. "Broadcasting, long-distance telephony, the talking film, and the gramophone," he says truly, "will make such standardisation possible, and even comparatively easy to establish." Anything else a language may be besides a "method of symbolising human thought" he considers as so little important that he can say:

> "If the keepers of our language maintain a die-hard attitude and succeed in preventing reasoned improvement, the result will, I suggest, be that language will be less and less used for intellectual and rational purposes, and relegated to an altogether inferior status as the symbolism of sentiment and small talk."

This is the only recognition Sir Richard gives to English Literature. He, too, proposes to use compulsion: he would suppress Mr. James Joyce, or, rather, the future die-hard of Mr. Joyce's kind:

> "I can see no alternative but that there should, eventually, be a censorship of words, and that the printing or use in public of such improper words should be forbidden."

[1] *The Need for Eugenic Reform*, Major Leonard Darwin.

It is no laughing matter: Sir Richard Paget does in some way represent enlightenment as against conservative inertia. On the one hand, the academic custodians of tradition are what they are. On the other, there is so strong a case to be made out for some such reform as Sir Richard Paget advocates. No one aware of the situation and concerned about the future of Shakespeare's language can view quite happily the interest taken by some of the most alert minds of our day in such a scheme as "Basic English."[1] This instrument, embodying the extreme of analytical economy, is, of course, intended for a limited use. But what hope is there that the limits will be kept? If "Basic English" proves as efficacious as it promises it will not remain a mere transition language for the Chinese. What an excellent instrument of education it would make, for instance, in the English-speaking countries! And, if hopes are fulfilled, the demand for literature in "Basic English" will grow to vast dimensions as Asia learns how to use this means of access to the West. It seems incredible that the English language as used in the West should not be affected, especially in America, where it is so often written as if it were not native to the writer, and where the general use of it is so little subject to control by sentimental conservatism. Mass-production and standardisation have not achieved their supreme triumph yet:

[1] See *Basic English*, C. K. Ogden, and *Carl and Anna in Basic English* (*Psyche Miniatures Series*).

"Meanwhile the president of the Radio Corporation of America proclaims an era at hand when 'the oldest and the newest civilisation will throb together at the same intellectual appeal, and to the same artistic emotions.'"[1]

We cannot be indifferent in the face of such possibilities. For, as we noted above, when we used the metaphor of "language" in defining culture we were using more than a metaphor. The most important part of this "language" is actually a matter of the use of words. Without the living subtlety of the finest idiom (which is dependent upon use) the heritage dies.[2] It is a measure of the desperateness of the situation that intelligent people, when, this is put to them, should be able to reply: "O, but you can go on using *your* language: what does it matter what the rest of the world does?" So difficult can it be for really alert and unprejudiced minds to-day to understand what it is that is being discussed: things have gone so far already.

The prospects of culture, then, are very dark. There is the less room for hope in that a standardised civilisation is rapidly enveloping the whole world. The glimpse of Russia that is permitted us does not afford the comfort that we are sometimes invited to find there. Anyone who has seen Eisenstein's

[1] *Middletown*, p. 268.

[2] "From the beginning civilisation has been dependent upon speech, for words are our chief link with the past and with one another and the channel of our spiritual inheritance. As the other vehicles of tradition, the family and the community, for example, are dissolved, we are forced more and more to rely upon language."—*Practical Criticism*, pp. 320–321.

film, *The General Line*, will appreciate the comment made by a writer in the *New Republic* (June 4, 1930) comparing it with an American film:

> "One fancies, thinking about these things, that America might well send *The Silent Enemy* to Russia and say, 'This is what living too long with too much machinery does to people. Think twice, before you commit yourselves irrevocably to the same course.'"

But it is vain to resist the triumph of the machine. It is equally vain to console us with the promise of a "mass culture" that shall be utterly new. It would, no doubt, be possible to argue that such a "mass culture" might be better than the culture we are losing, but it would be futile: the "utterly new" surrenders everything that can interest us.[1]

What hope, then, is there left to offer? The vague hope that recovery *must* come, somehow, in spite of all? Mr. I. A. Richards, whose opinion is worth more than most people's, seems to authorise hope: he speaks of "reasons for thinking that this century is in a cultural trough rather than upon a crest"; and says that "the situation is likely to get worse before it is better."[2] "Once the basic level has been reached," he suggests, "a slow climb back may be possible. That at least is a hope that may be reasonably entertained."[3] But it is a hope that

[1] ". . . indeed, this gentleman, taking the bull by the horns, proposes that we should for the future call industrialism culture, and then of course there can be no longer any misapprehension of their true character; and besides the pleasure of being wealthy and comfortable, they will have authentic recognition as vessels of sweetness and light."—*Culture and Anarchy*.

[2] *Practical Criticism*, p. 320. [3] *Ibid.*, p. 249.

looks very desperate in face of the downward acceleration described above, and it does not seem to point to any factor that might be counted upon to reverse the process.

Are we then to listen to Spengler's[1] (and Mr. Henry Ford's[2]) admonition to cease bothering about the inevitable future? That is impossible. Ridiculous, priggish and presumptuous as it may be, if we care at all about the issues we cannot help believing that, for the immediate future, at any rate, we have some responsibility. We cannot help clinging to some such hope as Mr. Richards offers; to the belief (unwarranted, possibly) that what we value most matters too much to the race to be finally abandoned, and that the machine will yet be made a tool.

It is for us to be as aware as possible of what is happening, and, if we can, to "keep open our communications with the future." 1930.

[1] "Up to now everyone has been at liberty to hope what he pleased about the future. Where there are no facts, sentiment rules. But henceforward it will be every man's business to inform himself of what *can* happen and therefore of what with the unalterable necessity of destiny and irrespective of personal ideals, hopes or desires, *will* happen."—*The Decline of the West*, Vol. I, p. 39.

[2] "But what of the future? Shall we not have over-production? Shall we not some day reach a point where the machine becomes all powerful, and the man of no consequence?

No man can say anything of the future. We need not bother about it. The future has always cared for itself in spite of our well-meant efforts to hamper it. If to-day we do the task we can best do, then we are doing all that we can do.

Perhaps we may over-produce, but that is impossible until the whole world has all its desires. And if that should happen, then surely we ought to be content."—*To-day and To-morrow*, HENRY FORD, pp. 272-273.

"THE LITERARY MIND"

MR. MAX EASTMAN, in the book[1] that bears the title at the head of this essay, presents an interesting case. It is of himself that I am thinking. For, while the case he propounds about "the literary mind" is too naïve and muddled in its complacent philistinism to be seriously discussed, he does indeed witness most impressively to the decay of literary culture. His book may be recommended as a representative document. He is "intellectual and a poet," he tells us. Yet he can point to the almost complete disappearance of serious critical journals in the last few decades as evidence that we have improved. They have disappeared, he thinks, because Science has put out of date the literary culture they represented. We know nowadays where to go for "verified statements," and those who contend that literature matters vitally to civilisation "are fighting for the right of literary men to talk loosely and yet be taken seriously in a scientific age."

Now "literary men"—moralising dons, humanists and others—have indeed been guilty of a great deal of "loose talk." But the critic who proposes to discuss a "classical movement" led by "Allen Tate, Ezra Pound, T. S. Eliot, Ivor Winters, Edith Sitwell, Robert Graves, Laura Riding" convicts himself of a

[1] *The Literary Mind*, Max Eastman.

looseness that dimisses him with the loosest. Anyone who offers such a list must be pronounced not to know what he is talking about. Mr. Eastman simply cannot see the difference in intellectual status between Mr. Eliot and Miss Sitwell, except that he finds Miss Sitwell more discussible. In poetry he positively prefers her. *Ash-Wednesday* he refers to as an "oily puddle of emotional noises," but "Edith Sitwell is, in my opinion, the most gifted of the modernist poets." The late Arnold Bennett, it will be remembered, had a like preference. The reason is simple: it is that Miss Sitwell is simple, and offers her admirers, with "modernist" garnishings, what they expect to find in poetry—sentimental reveries, reminiscences of childhood, and so on. For criticism she does not exist, either as a poet or a critic.

But no suspicion of his total incapacity troubles the assurance with which Mr. Eastman puts "humane letters" in their place. "Modernist" poetry is unintelligible, he explains, because "Science has withdrawn intellect from literature," and has left the poet nothing more serious to do than to engineer, as a defensive bluff, a "revolt against meaningful language." This innocent self-exposure, this complacent illiteracy, if it were merely amusing, would not be worth dwelling on. But what public can one count on to find it amusing? If one says that it is as absurd to defend as to attack "modernist" poetry—that there is no "modernist" poetry, but only two or three modern poets—what public will recognise a platitude? Mr. Eastman is an American, but here in England Mr. Eliot's poetry is explained over the wireless by Mr. Harold Nicolson, and our most intelligent weekly is, where literary criticism is concerned, a stronghold of anti-highbrow prejudice.

Mr. Eastman is right, though the case that he enforces is not what he intended: the tradition of literary culture is dead, or nearly so. If it was Science that killed it, it was not in the way that Mr. Eastman explains, but by being the engine of the social changes that have virtually broken continuity. The standards that, maintained in a living tradition, constituted a surer taste than any individual as such can pretend to, have gone with the tradition; there is now no centre and no authority, so that Mr. Eastman, Mr. Nicolson, Mr. Priestley or Mr. Walpole can assume authority without being in the eyes of the world ridiculous.

Mr. Eastman of course does not grieve over the loss, one of its manifestations being that he cannot realise it. For what I have spoken of as the literary tradition was more than literary, and its dissolution has bearings outside the field of mere adornment and amenity. To start with a limited and immediately pertinent one: what, as exhibited in *The Literary Mind*, is wrong with Mr. Eastman's *intelligence?*—That he is deficient in taste and sensibility is plain. My present point is that these deficiencies are associated with others of a kind that he could, perhaps, be brought to recognise. By a little analysis it should be possible to bring home to him that he is deficient on the side of intelligence. He maintains an air of incisiveness and intellectual rigour, but his writing is both loose (to use his own term) and blunt. Not only does he use such key words as "experience," "interpretation," and "meaning" with an uncritical looseness, but, apart from (or rather accentuated in) localisable confusions and fallacies there is a pervasive debility, a lack of tension, outline and edge, in his thinking. The point might be made by saying that he has none of that sensitiveness of intelligence without which all apparent vigour of thought is illusory. And when such a phrase as "sensitiveness of intelligence" suggests itself it begins to appear that the relation between "intelligence" and "sensibility" is not the simple distinction that is readily assumed.

In fact, Mr. Eastman's defect of sensibility is a defect of intelligence. This becomes plain if we say that he lacks fineness of perception, though there is a great deal more to be said. What we diagnose in expression, as inadequacy in the use of words, goes back to an inadequacy behind the words, an inadequacy of experience; a failure of something that should have pressed upon them and controlled them to sharp significance. Mr. Eastman does not offer himself, at any rate in *The Literary Mind*, as a poet, and so it is not required of him that his prose should evoke the concrete particulars of immediate experience. But his undertaking is such that without a fine sensibility, without a discriminating awareness, and without an ability to discern and fix differences of quality and degree, he is without his essential data. A certain fidelity to concrete particulars *is* required of him. And it may be hazarded of all thinking, however abstract, that is likely to interest those of us who are preoccupied with the problems of living, that the criticism of it concerns its fidelity to concrete particulars and the quality of these. No easy distinction between intelligence and sensibility comes to hand here. Of good prose, in so far as it is abstract and general, it may be said that its virtues are a matter of the negative presence of the concrete and particular; it is not merely absence, but exclusion, an exclusion felt as a pressure. Exclusion implies a firm and subtle grasp; to exclude, the writer must have experienced, perceived and realised. Mr. Eliot is a major poet, and Mr. Eliot's prose is among the most finely and purely prosaic ever written; it is the efficient instrument of a fine critical intelligence.

The psychologist (if he bothered) might comment that to attempt to pass off such terms as "intelligence" and "sensibility" in this way without analysis and definition, is an amusingly innocent and impotent procedure. The reader I have in mind may, while agreeing that my use of the terms is plain enough for my purpose, comment that a truism could be enunciated with less fuss. I hope in this essay to show why I think the point worth insisting on, and worth developing at this non-technical level, in spite of the risks.

To begin with, let the reader I have supposed recall the reception that any serious attempt to apply critical intelligence to poetry almost universally meets with. If the critic is complimented on being intelligent, it is commonly with the implication that he would be a better critic if he were less so: "intelligent" becomes, by an imperceptible transition, "too intellectual." The appreciation of poetry, we are told, is a matter of "feeling" or "insight," not of "willed intellectual effort." A related judgment is that the "Cambridge School" (whatever that may be) conceives poetry too much as a "deliberate intellectual criticism of life." I am not denying that certain wrong approaches to poetry may fairly be described as too intellectual (to err in such ways is to err by not being intelligent enough). My point is that any serious attempt to apply intelligence to poetry has to face prejudice against the "intellectual" approach.

The reception of Mr. Empson's *Seven Types of Ambiguity* illustrated this. Reviewers who nerved themselves to tackle the book (it was shamefully neglected) commonly paid tribute to the author's remarkable intelligence, but contrived to suggest that it was employed, at the best, in an arduous and interesting, but gratuitous, form of exercise which had little bearing upon "appreciation"; for those of us who are no good at mathematics and science, it would be hinted, there is still a field, requiring no cerebral tension, where we need not feel inferior. Now I will not deny that Mr. Empson's zest has sometimes kept him going too long and too ingeniously in the pursuit of ambiguities; but for the most part his analysis is simply the appropriate, critical, and very unusually efficient application of intelligence to poetry. Partly it is a matter of noting and registering with conscious attention what was implicit in our response. But also (and this is the report of everyone with whom I have discussed the book) Mr. Empson convicts us again and again of having missed something essential in the passages we thought we knew—of having failed to respond properly. It was an illusion that, though we might not be given to "intellectual" analysis, we were, as persons of taste, able to "appreciate." And was the deficiency in our response one of sensibility or intelligence?

"Intelligence" is the word that, with my eye upon Mr. Max Eastman, I want at the moment to stress. Mr. Empson's book serves to bring home how largely and in what ways literary criticism is a matter of intelligence. The bearings of this conclusion upon Mr. Eastman's case are well brought out by this admirable passage from Mr. Ezra Pound's perverse, but fruitfully provocative, pamphlet *How to Read*:

"Has literature a function in the state, in the aggregation of humans, in the republic, in the *res publica* . . . ? It has.

". . . It has to do with the clarity and vigour of 'any and every' thought and opinion. It has to do with maintaining the very cleanliness of the tools, the health of the very matter of thought itself. Save in the rare and limited instances of invention in the plastic arts, or in mathematics, the individual cannot think and communicate his thought, the governor and legislator cannot act effectively or frame his laws, without words, and the solidity and validity of these words is in the care of the damned and despised *literati*. When their work goes rotten—by that I do not mean when they express indecorous thoughts—but when their very medium, the very essence of their work, the application of word to thing goes rotten, i.e., becomes slushy and inexact, or excessive or bloated, the whole machinery of social and of individual thought and order goes to pot."

This is well said. Literary criticism has a correspondingly high function, and literary study, so far from producing the "literary mind" conceived by Mr. Eastman, should be the best possible training for intelligence—for free, unspecialised, general intelligence, which there has never at any time been enough of, and which we are peculiarly in need of to-day. This is not to say that literary criticism should not be specialised, in the sense that its practice should be controlled by a strict conception of its special nature and methods. Indeed, the more one realises its importance in the education of general intelligence, the more is one concerned for strictness of conception and practice.

But to demand such strictness in any field is to invite the charge of dogmatic intolerance and narrowness. It will not, for instance, do to refer as matter of commonplace to the almost complete absence of profitable Shakespeare criticism after two centuries of what must, for want of another word, be called critical activity. It may be said that, as a rule, the more respectable the critic the more deplorable the result: if, of the academics, Bradley is the best, he is the worst. How long has Hamlet been down from Wittenberg? How many children had Lady Macbeth? Those *Appendices* of Bradley's are, perhaps, now commonly thought odd, and if they don't bring home the preposterousness of his approach (which is the orthodox), argument hardly will. There may sometimes be uses for the detective, psychological, moral, philosophical or acrostical approaches, but they are not literary criticism, and unless controlled by literary criticism they are vicious. Of course, where Shakespeare is concerned, literary criticism needs its auxiliaries, but it is still the essential approach; yet, though we have the auxiliaries, their *raison d'être* (for want of which they themselves are usually defective) hardly exists. The critical approach to a Shakespeare play will not consider it as primarily a pattern of characters (or persons), with their "psychologies," in action and interaction, but will remember that *we* form these by abstraction from Shakespeare's words—that he didn't create persons, but put words together—and it will apply this principle or truism in a strenuous critical method. This does not mean that the critic will not have to consider character, action and moral questions, but that his concern with these will be a relevant one and so profitable. Bradley's is, as a rule, more or less subtly irrelevant, and has little to do with the appreciation of Shakespeare. His method is not intelligent enough, and, to reverse my earlier stress, the defect of intelligence is a default on the part of sensibility; a failure to keep closely enough in touch with responses to particular arrangements of words.

The need for a strict conception of literary criticism and for a rigorous discipline in practice will perhaps be assented to as obvious where Shakespeare is concerned. Something that may be called in a respectable sense the "literary mind"—a mind with a special literary training—is obviously in place here. It is equally so, if less obviously, in dealing with certain writers, poets or prose-artists, who are not pure artists, but invite the discussion of doctrine or ideas as such; by intelligence, that is, apart from sensibility, or apart, at any rate, from the trained sensibility of the literary critic. Wordsworth is an instance. He invites us to discuss his "philosophy." It is disastrous to accept. Or rather, the only profitable approach to the "philosophy" is by way of strict literary criticism. Arnold's word is perhaps even more apt than he intended; the philosophy is an illusion. It simply does not exist to be discussed as such. If you find anything to discuss, to a great extent you put it there yourself. "To a great extent" is a necessary concession: that Wordsworth *had* ideas is not an illusion. But the only way to fix anything for discussion in the shifting verbosities of his abstract "thinking" is to start from the concrete and never lose touch with it. What is successful as poetry is obviously "there"; its abstractable implications, or those encouraged by a general knowledge of Wordsworth, may be coaxed out as far as seems discreet into the Wordsworthian philosophic fog and the poetry made the solid nucleus for such organisation in terms of "thought" as seems worth attempting. But we ought never to forget that Wordsworth matters as a "thinker" only (if at all) because he is a poet.

The same rule and consequent procedure apply to D. H. Lawrence, and in his case, perhaps, it will be more readily perceived that there is reason for insisting on them. For Lawrence's "thought" bears upon issues that are urgent to us and have been much in debate. He was a "prophet," but it is only because he was an artist of genius that his prophecy matters. But for that genius he would have demanded no more attention as a thinker than the mob of anthroposophists, Keyserlings, and hierophants of psycho-mythopœia. His gift lay, not in thinking, but in experiencing, and in fixing and evoking in words the feelings and perceptions that seemed to him most significant. Lawrence's commentary on experience, his doctrine, must be approached by way of the concrete, the successful art; criticism of the doctrine cannot be separated from judgments concerning literary success or failure;

discussion, to be intelligent, must be controlled by the critical sensibility. There is no other way of maintaining relevance, of fixing anything in Lawrence for examination, of ensuring that discussion or elucidation shall not be merely a matter of using Lawrence as an opportunity of expounding something of one's own. I had insisted on this approach by literary criticism in an essay on Lawrence and so was gratified as well as depressed when Mr. Middleton Murry confirmed me. For, in writing *Son of Woman*, he was so interested in the doctrine and so convinced that he understood it and Lawrence that he did not trouble to apply such a discipline as I have contended for. And *Son of Woman* is another book about Mr. Middleton Murry. As such it is interesting. But it has the appearance of being a book about Lawrence and in so far as it passes for such it is vicious. However, perhaps the pervasive tone and the constant implication that Mr. Murry has the key and the measure—the Absolute—in his pocket, give warning enough to all but the simple-minded. But the book remains an apt illustration for my argument, and not the less so because when Mr. Murry does make judgments of literary criticism he shows himself, for one who has been so fine a critic, almost incredibly defective in sensibility. He says, for instance, of *The Plumed Serpent*: "It is Lawrence's greatest work of 'art.'" Now to the critical sensibility *The Plumed Serpent* is notable among Lawrence's novels for betraying by a certain strain, a falsity, a forced tone (capable of analysis), that Lawrence does not really feel what he wants to feel, that he does not believe what he is trying to believe. Here was an opportunity to open an indubitably relevant critique, which might in due course have pointed out, among other things, that the terrible monotony of *The Plumed Serpent* (this is not to deny the marks of genius in it) is a comment on Lawrence's prophecy. But whatever Mr. Murry's intelligence may have been doing, it was not a critic's sensibility he chose to employ here; and the defect of sensibility shows as a defect of intelligence.

It should now be plain that the "literary mind"—the intelligence trained as it can be only in the study of literature—has work to do outside the field of literary "appreciation." Why, for instance, has the debate about "Humanism" been so depressing? The issues it handles belong to a realm where it is extremely difficult to do anything at all—to say anything that advances discussion; for the handling, intelligence of the kind indicated is an essential qualification. Its absence, the defect of sensibility, is manifested in the debile abstraction of that prose with which we are all too familiar. There may be no gross fallacies; but without a sustained, tense and living relation with the concrete, with the particulars of experience, the intellectual respectability and the erudition are barren. Many Humanists (and anti-Humanists) seem incapable of particular experience at all. D. H. Lawrence had a genius for it, and his importance as a "thinker" is that he could command the concrete by creative art. One does not criticise

Humanists (or anti-Humanists) for lacking this gift. Their undertaking is not creative; but it does nevertheless demand a discriminating capacity for experience, and an ability to keep in close touch with the concrete by means of the critical intelligence. So it was a damning comment on Professor Irving Babbitt and his associates when, in a manifesto published in the *New Republic*, they were challenged to produce their record with regard to contemporary letters: it is, of course, one of complacent obtuseness.

We have in England erudite and laborious essayists who invite the same kind of comment. Mr. McEachran, for instance, is distinguished, not only by his comparative modesty of tone and his brevity, but also by the frankness with which he exhibits something like a complete lack of interest in literature, music and art. That he knows nothing of music he explicitly does not consider a disqualification, for he argues that it is better to be unmusical (see *The Civilised Man*, pp. 132 ff.). The plastic arts he does suppose himself to be interested in; but how complete an illusion this is may be gathered from his finding it possible to argue (the extraction does him no injustice) that "because a civilised man is higher than a savage, a statue portraying him is a greater thing than a statue of a savage, however beautifully executed, and this because a civilised man is higher than a savage" (*The Civilised Man*, p. 117). As for his degree of literary education, it is fairly suggested by the way in which he argues from *Faust*: "The task of the second part, which from the point of view of poetry is inferior to it on the whole, was to fill out some of these defects" [of the first part, which doesn't suit Mr. McEachran's argument at all]: "to present Goethe's outlook as not finally diverse from the one we have said to be human" (*The Civilised Man*, p. 70). The assumption that poetical inferiority has no bearing on the argument is characteristic of the type of thought: an abstract "outlook" that in its loose generality can be attributed to Goethe is all the writer is interested in. Here we have localised for inspection the pervasive weakness that makes such books as *The Civilised Man*, however erudite and careful, so barren and impotent.

Mr. Lawrence Hyde is a critic of Humanism, but his book, *The Prospects of Humanism*, exhibits the same weakness. He appears to be entirely without critical sensibility. He finds that, in the sphere of literature, "there is a never-ending stream of biography, criticism, and fiction, all incredibly interesting and readable, all artistically produced, all written with a clearness, a vivacity, a subtle provocativeness, which makes them almost irresistible to any person of imagination and taste" (*The Prospects of Humanism*, p. 126). He speaks of "the remarkable amount of distinguished and sincere work which is appearing at the present time. The standard of execution is incredibly high; every month there appear a whole row of books, each of which represents the best which the talented author has in him (or her; particularly her)" (*The Prospects of Humanism*, p. 155). This innocence is so amiable that one would rather not have had to point out how completely it damns Mr. Hyde as a thinker. It is not unrelated to the quality that enables him to discuss the "thought" of Mr. J. C. Powys seriously.

Then there is Mr. Montgomery Belgion, who is not amiable, but as "a steady contributor to the *Criterion*" (see the April issue), insists on some notice. His function in the commonwealth, he feels, is to expose current confusions and fallacies by rigorous intellectual analysis; and it would not be difficult to expose Mr. Belgion's confusions and fallacies by the method he affects. But few sensitive readers of *The Human Parrot* will bother to do that; it is so plain that Mr. Belgion's is not a sensitive intelligence. He does not hazard himself much in the field of literary judgment, but he leaves no room for doubt about the quality of his critical sensibility. For all his air of nice precision his tools are soft and blunt.

I have already referred to the relation between Mr. Eliot's poetic gift and the quality of intelligence exhibited in his literary criticism. It is in place to note that the distinction of his intelligence appears as plainly when he applies it to general questions. Whether one agree with him or not, it is impossible not to see that he is in a very different class from Professor Irving Babbitt and Messrs. McEachran, Hyde and Belgion: he really does something with his words.

But up to now I have narrowed the issue too much. To return to Mr. Max Eastman: in the deficiencies that we have discussed he does not, we see, stand alone; but in his attitude to Science he is, at this date, remarkable. Few scientists would make the claims for it that he does. He believes with implicit faith that it will settle all our problems for us. In short, he lives still in the age of H. G. Wells. "And nobody," he says scornfully, "is going to consult humane letters about the mortal problems of our industrial civilisation; he is going to consult sociology and economics." But sociology and economics, if they are to be sciences, can give no adequate answer to the questions that are waived by that phrase, "the standard of living," as the economists use it. Our problems cannot be settled without reference to the ends of life, without decisions as to what kind of life is desirable, and it is an elementary fallacy to suppose that such decisions can be left to Science. But "humane letters," though they may have no authority in the province of "certified facts," have a good deal of authority in the question of what, in the long run, humanity is likely to find a satisfactory way of life. One way of indicating the deficiency as prophets of Mr. Bernard Shaw, Lord Russell and Mr. H. G. Wells (Mr. Eliot's disrespect towards them shocks Mr. Eastman) is to say that they have missed, or are incapable of, the education that can be got through "humane letters."

What I have in mind is no mere training of the

individual sensibility such as, for the not incapable, a course of practical criticism could provide. Indeed the problem cannot be adequately thought of as one of the "culture" of individuals. No doubt if Mr. Wells could read Shakespeare and had some knowledge of Dante his sense of value would be finer. But a concern for "culture" in that sense is inadequate to the issues. It is to the culture that transcends the individual as the language he inherits transcends him that we come back; to the culture that has decayed with tradition. The standards maintained in such a tradition, I remarked near the beginning of this essay, constitute a surer taste than any individual can pretend to. And it is not merely a matter of literary taste. The culture in question, which is not, indeed, identical with literary tradition but which will hardly survive it, is a sense of relative value and a memory—such wisdom as constitutes the residuum of the general experience. It lives only in individuals, but individuals can live without it; and where they are without it they do not know what they miss. And the world, troubled as it is, is unaware of what is gone. So nearly complete is the gap in cultural consciousness that to-day those who win attention by their disinterested concern for the future of the race are mostly of the type of Mr. Wells. Mr. A. L. Rowse's *Politics and the Younger Generation* is representative. Though it mentions most of the names that are current to-day as having "culture" value, it betrays an essential illiteracy; the author, that is, in so far as reading means ability to approach literature, shows that he cannot read. And to this illiteracy relates, in the ways suggested, the blurred muddle of the writing, a certain unnecessary grossness of manners and a disabling impercipience where the problems of the "standard of living" are concerned.

To revive or replace a decayed tradition is a desperate undertaking; the attempt may seem futile. But perhaps there will be some agreement that no social or political movement unrelated to such an attempt could engage one's faith and energy. The more immediate conclusions would seem to bear upon education. No one aware of the problem will entertain easy hopes, for, inevitably, the machinery of education works in with the process of the modern world; and in the absence of standards, how can we start a reverse process? Something in the nature of luck is needed; the luck, let us say, that provides a centre of stimulus and a focus of energy at some university. All that falls under the head of "English" there becomes, then, in spite of Mr. H. G. Wells, of supreme importance.

Unhappily, the connotations of the term "academic" are of ill augury: the concern for "tradition" that I have in mind will not be that commonly associated with formal education. Everything must start from and be related to the training of sensibility, that kind of training in which Mr. Richards was a pioneer. Then with some hope the study of literary history—of periods, developments and relations—may be directed to producing a real grasp of the idea of living tradition. Sensibility and the idea of tradition—both concerns are essential. The latter is inseparable from the former; otherwise we have the academic sterility, the Humanist manipulation of the barren idea, the inability to conceive tradition as a matter of organic life. And no one could propose to foster the idea of living tradition by a study of literature that should ignore the present. It is when we come to the present that a serious interest in literature becomes inevitably something more; and a serious attempt of the kind under discussion would associate education in "English" with the study of the background of literature, its cultural and sociological conditions and bearings, present and past, of cultural history and so on.

As for the schools, it seems a particularly vicious waste that intelligent men should have to enter teaching as a *pis aller*, with little hope but to become spiritless tenders of the machine. That, for those who teach English, there is, or might be, a function commanding enthusiasm I have implied above. For the training of sensibility should begin at school, and would command in both teacher and pupils a deeper interest than Verity's notes. And a good deal might be done to cultivate a critical awareness of contemporary civilisation. Many who have to make their living by the machine will smile sadly or cynically at these suggestions. And yet there are some opportunities. Even now, without the impulsion and support that I have desiderated and without good books, men are contriving to do valuable work on these lines.

An essay on the "literary mind" has developed, significantly (if I have not divagated), into this. The reader may smile at my portentousness. I do not, at any rate, suppose myself to have suggested a complete programme for the regeneration of mankind. My essay is an answer to the challenge represented by Mr. Eastman's book. As one devoted to the study and teaching of literature I have asked myself: why do I think this devotion, in an age of "crises," a worthy one? My answer, if not modest, is as honest and as serious as I can make it.

1932.

WHAT'S WRONG WITH CRITICISM?

A REPRESENTATIVE set[1] of books of contemporary criticism is at any rate an occasion for the inquiry proposed above. That literary criticism is not in a healthy state we all—readers of this journal, or those, at least, in sympathy with the undertaking—assume; the undertaking explicitly affirms it. But perhaps we assume a consensus too easily: it is of the essence of the plight that the plight can be questioned. As of taste, so of criticism; we must expect to be assured with Olympian dispassionateness that it always has been in a bad state and always will be. Such dispassionateness is probably invincible. Yet that the argument should be found impressive represents one of the most desperate of the conditions that we have to deal with, and the challenge to cogency of statement should sometimes be taken up.

No one is going to assert that criticism was ever in a satisfactory state. Just what, then, is peculiarly and so desperately wrong to-day? Why all this fuss?

One may start, paradoxically, by asserting that this age will be remarkable in literary history for its achievement in criticism. The histories of literary criticism contain a great many names, but how many critics are there who have made any

[1] *Poetry and the Criticism of Life*, H. W. Garrod. *Variety of Ways*, Bonamy Dobrée. *Criticism*, Desmond MacCarthy.

difference to one—improved one's apparatus, one's equipment, one's efficiency as a reader? At least two of them are of our time: Mr. Eliot and Mr. Richards; it is a very large proportion indeed of the total. Mr. Richards has improved the instruments of analysis, and has consolidated and made generally accessible the contribution of Coleridge. Mr. Eliot has not only refined the conception and the methods of criticism; he has put into currency decisive re-organising and re-orientating ideas and valuations. The stimulus of these two very dissimilar forces has already made itself felt, and there is no reason to suppose that Mr. Empson's book will prove to be the only important critical work produced by their juniors.

But all this does not affect the conviction expressed in the second sentence of this essay. That this is so one might attempt to enforce by adducing Professor Garrod's *Poetry and the Criticism of Life*. Professor Garrod says of Coleridge: "The appeal of his poetry is strong with me; and the appeal of the man. But just those qualities which make a critic he seems to me to lack." And that disposes of Coleridge. It will be readily and rightly guessed that just those qualities which make a critic are what the rest of the book shows Professor Garrod to lack: yet it was respectfully reviewed by respected authority. But evidence of this kind is not to be seriously urged. There is long-established precedent for Professor Garrod and his reception, and his book does not really raise the important issues.

Nor does Mr. Bonamy Dobrée's *Variety of Ways*. One might set it over against Professor Garrod's book as showing that academic criticism is not necessarily unprofitable. Mr. Dobrée is not merely elegant, and such scholarly essays as his on Congreve perform a function, though his treatment of rhythm and style—indeed of all he handles—would have been more profitable if his scholarship and taste had been served by a better analytic equipment. But this is not the debate intended in the question, "What's wrong with criticism?"; we cannot start from this text.

It is the third book, Mr. Desmond MacCarthy's, that really raises the issues. For Mr. MacCarthy is not a professor of poetry or a scholar or a specialist, but a professional critic, a journalist; in him criticism undertakes its essential function of keeping an educated body of taste and opinion alive to the age, of testing, nourishing and refining the currency of contemporary culture. And that there is still in some sense somewhere something like an educated body of taste and opinion the intelligence and limitations of Mr. MacCarthy's *Criticism* together show. For nowhere does it give evidence of any subtlety of first-hand judgment. In all the testing cases—in dealing with Donnè and David Garnett, for instance—he is conventional and superficial. D. H. Lawrence he compares with Carlyle and T. S. Eliot with Browning, leaving the stress on the likeness; no one intelligently interested in either could have done that. Mr. MacCarthy, then, is not an original critic; he is the journalist-middleman of cultivated talk.

On this estimate he does at any rate testify to the existence of a certain cultivated *milieu* where there is an active interest in literature. But his significance for this inquiry lies in his distinction—for he is distinguished, if not quite in the way his reputation intends. In the serious pursuit of his function he enjoys something like a lonely eminence. Who else is there? In a healthy state we should have at least twenty journalist-critics of his quality, whereas if we look round we can see only the *confrérie* of the weeklies and the Sunday papers. The distinction so indicated, moreover, is one that the bulk of his readers cannot be counted on to appreciate to the full. Who, if not they, form the *élite* that follows the reviewing in "our more elegant weeklies" (for the reviewing here, whatever may be the case with the accompaniment to the Sunday advertising, does appear to be taken seriously by such educated class as we have?)

Here, then, we have come to what is radically wrong with criticism. The public that makes any show of interest in literature is only a small minority, and though there may be behind Mr. MacCarthy a circle actively and intelligently interested, it is a tiny minority of a minority, which, for all the effect it has as representing generally operative standards, might as well not exist. And where there is no nucleus of an educated public representing such standards the function of criticism has fallen into abeyance, and no amount of improvement in the apparatus and technique will restore it. It becomes impossible even to get the plight recognised. My argument, for instance (I lapse appropriately into the first person), will, except to those who find it obvious, seem for the most part an arbitrary tissue of arrogant dogmatisms.

It is more than the function of criticism that has fallen into abeyance. To those who take a serious interest in literature it must often seem as if their interest were curiously irrelevant to the modern world; curiously, because a serious interest in literature starts from the present and assumes that literature matters, in the first place at any rate, as the consciousness of the age. If a literary tradition does not keep itself alive here, in the present, not merely in new creation, but as a pervasive influence upon feeling, thought and standards of living (it is time we challenged the current use of this phrase), then it must be pronounced to be dying or dead. Indeed, it seems hardly likely that, when this kind of influence becomes negligible, creation will long persist. In any case, a consciousness maintained by an insulated minority and without effect upon the powers that rule the world has lost its function. And this describes well enough the existing state of affairs. To put it in more particular terms, no one interested in poetry can suppose that if all the serious poets now writing died within the year the newspapers would register any noticeable shock. The world is not interested;

and this lack of interest must seem to those concerned about culture more frightening than hostility.

The world, it will be retorted, has something else to be interested in; those who see the desperate need for action, political and other, can have no concern to spare for the state of poetry and literary criticism. The need for political action few will be inclined to deny. But it seems pertinent to inquire the worth of political action or theory that is not directed towards realising some idea of satisfactory living. I do not assert that traditional culture and literary tradition are identical, but their relation is such that those who are aware of it will not expect one to survive without the other; and it would seem romantic to expect that an adequate idea will issue out of amnesia—out of a divorce from the relevant experience of the race.

For some, of course, the problem is simple; inherited art and culture are bourgeois and must be replaced. Upon this philosophy I can hardly hope to make an impression, but I can hope, for most who are likely to read me, to have made clear the nature of my concern about the death of the literary tradition and the state of criticism—that it is not a concern for the prestige of a minority as such.

The phrase "minority culture" appears to have gained currency. What does not appear to be equally current is the realisation that a genuine concern for "minority culture" cannot be satisfaction with it. The more one cares about the values it preserves, the more clearly one realises the function it represents, the less likely is one to be drawn towards the pleasures of Pharisaism.

There are, of course, the pleasures of pessimism, and they have no doubt been suspected of complicity in my assertion about the newspapers and the hypothetical death of all our poets. But the assertion was critically sober, and the stress judicial. For, as a matter of fact, the decay of the literary tradition is less conclusively manifested in the grosser absurdities of, say, the *Observer* (which after all are notorious) than in the more respectable absurdities of our most respected anthologies, with their scores of modern poets—Professor Lascelles Abercrombie recently presented a drove of forty. These anthologies are not, among Mr. MacCarthy's public (let us say), a byword for fatuity; they exhibit fairly the state of contemporary taste. The standards that, maintained in a living tradition, should have made them impossible have vanished, for the tradition has vanished, and the conventional respect for poetry of the cultivated remains, in general, purely conventional, uninformed by tradition—"traditional," that is, in the bad sense.

Poetry, then, though it may still be examined on at school, has ceased to matter; it is taken, if at all, on authority. Where, on the other hand, the world takes interest, authority—the authority vested in tradition—has disappeared, as was foreseen by the late Sir Edmund Gosse forty years ago:

"One danger which I have long foreseen from the

spread of democratic sentiment is that of the traditions of literary taste, the canons of literature, being reversed with success by a popular vote. Up to the present time, in all parts of the world, the masses of uneducated or semi-educated persons, who form the vast majority of the race, have been content to acknowledge their traditional supremacy. Of late there have seemed to me to be certain signs, especially in America, of a revolt of the mob against our literary masters. . . . If literature is to be judged by a plebiscite and if the plebs recognises its powers, it will certainly by degrees cease to support reputations which give it no pleasure and which it cannot comprehend. The revolution against taste, once begun, will land us in irreparable chaos."[1]

Skimming through *The Life and Letters of Sir Edmund Gosse* one cannot help reflecting that he himself was a portent. He had, it appears, no qualification for authority except a belief in his right to it. This was sublime: "You are a poet of a high order," we find him writing to Mr. J. C. Squire, "and a mind in curiously close sympathy with me. I feel myself singularly in tune with you. I understand exactly what you say. It is so rare.... You will make a great name!" (And there are elsewhere in the book appreciations of Mr. Squire that deserve to become anthology-pieces.) His inability to see what is in front of him is sometimes almost incredible: he cultivates André Gide and finds Mr. E. M. Forster's *Howard's End*, that most maidenly, most transparently innocent, of books, "sensational, dirty, and affected." His critical

[1] "What is a Great Poet?" (1889), in *Questions at Issue.*

F

incapacity, sometimes comic, was always complete. And yet his success was complete too; he imposed himself and became an institution, the embodiment of critical authority. It looks as if the absence of standards that I have been deploring is no new thing. Nevertheless there is an important difference between the age of Edmund Gosse and the age of Arnold Bennett. The standards in Gosse's time may not have been generally operative among the "cultivated," but respect for them was. Nothing else can explain his ascendency: he stood for the taste and learning that, being above the general level, made it possible for the common man to hope to improve himself. But a tradition that allows itself to be embodied in a Gosse is obviously in danger.

Civilisation advanced. The triumph of "democratic sentiment" that Gosse foresaw was brought about by forces that he does not appear to have noticed. Mass-production, standardisation, levelling-down—these three terms convey succinctly, what has happened. Machine-technique has produced change in the ways of life at such a rate that there has been something like a breach of continuity; sanctions have decayed; and, in any case, the standards of mass-production (for mass-production conditions now govern the supply of literature) are not those of tradition. Instead of conventional respect for traditional standards we have the term "highbrow"; indeed, such remains of critical standards as a desperate and scattered minority may now fight for can hardly be called traditional, for the tradition has dissolved: the centre—Arnold's "centre of intelligent and urbane spirit," which, in spite of his plaints, we can see by comparison to have existed in his day—has vanished. Instead we have the Book Society, Ltd., recommending "worth-while" books with the psychological resources of modern publicity, one of the most valuable of which is the term "high-brow."

It is, then, vain to hope that standards will somehow re-establish themselves in the higgling of the market; the machinery of civilisation works unceasingly to obliterate the very memory of them. What then can be done? In despair one toys with desperate recourses: would it be of any use, before it is too late and oblivion sets in, to try to focus what remains of tradition in a "central authority representing higher culture and sound judgment"—to try whether an organ can be found, capable of the function that Arnold assigned to academies? "Such an effort," Arnold reminds us, "to set up a recognised authority, imposing on us a high standard in matters of intellect and taste, has many enemies in human nature." These enemies are now, to a degree that Arnold can hardly have foreseen, invested with power and conscious of virtue. Yet there are friends too—the need for such a standard is also in human nature—and perhaps the extremity of the case will rally them to the effort.

And then one remembers Sir Edmund Gosse: there we have the kind of mind that gets into academies. There is also the academic mind of the more respectable order represented by Professor Lascelles Abercrombie. Professor Abercrombie, writing on Literary Criticism in a recent *Outline of Modern Knowledge* (a production symptomatic of the times), devoted a third of his space to Aristotle and a proportionate amount to Longinus, and in his bibliography mentioned at least one bad and several insignificant books, but neither Mr. Richards nor Mr. Eliot. Still, the article is scholarly, and there might be something to be said for this kind of academic mind if only it could be brought into touch with what is alive.

Someone may by now have remembered that there is a Royal Society of Literature in being. Founded by George IV, it is already venerable: might not something be done to establish a recognised "centre of intelligent and urbane spirit" here? The Society is not notorious; no one, except its members, seems to know much about it. Readers of the *Times Literary Supplement,* however, will remember to have seen at intervals long and respectful reviews of certain volumes called *Essays by Divers Hands.* The hands are those of Fellows of the Royal Society of Literature.

If one hunts down the books in a library one has to brace oneself before dipping, they look so dull. Yet they do contain light reading. For instance, one may have the luck to take down the volume (1923) in which Mr. Alfred Noyes discourses on *Some Characteristics of Contemporary Literature:* "In the current number of the *Quarterly Review* there is a review—an exceedingly able review—of a recently published novel, which, I say without hesitation, and without the slightest fear that anyone here who has seen it will disagree with me, is the foulest that ever found its way into print." After the moralist the literary critic: "The technical quality of the writing is beneath contempt." Mr. Joyce is not even original; in realistic audacity he was forestalled by Tennyson in *Locksley Hall.* (Of *In Memoriam*, by the way, we are told: "It is probably the greatest elegy in any language, not because this or that authority says so, but demonstrably.") We are not, then, surprised to find that Mr. Noyes stands for tradition, and does not mince his words: "All over the English-speaking world this hunt"—represented, we gather, by Mr. Joyce and Mr. Eliot—"for an easier way in technique has been accompanied by a lowering of the standards in every direction. This quality of the thought and the emotion has been incredibly cheapened, and the absence of any fixed and central principles has led to an appalling lack of discrimination. Literary judgments in many cases have become purely arbitrary." And Mr. Noyes indicates his fellow-Paladins: ". . . The desire to break the continuity of our tradition has been fought by Mr. Edmund Gosse with the weapon of an irony as delicate as that of Anatole France. Critics of a later generation like Mr. Clutton Brock, Mr. J. C. Squire, Mr. Robert Lynd have also steadily sought to maintain a just balance between the old and the new."

Mr. Squire and Mr. Lynd, a defender of tradition in any serious sense would have to point out, have been among the most subtle and successful democratisers of standards. And it is comment enough on the academic conception of tradition—which is, of course, what Mr. Noyes stands for—to point to the company it keeps. In the Royal Society of Literature there is, for instance, Dean Inge, in whom, no doubt, in spite of the differing communions, Mr. Noyes finds a kindred spirit. Dean Inge, too, stands to the defence of technique against literary Bolshevism. He prescribes (1922) classical metres for English poetry: "We want laws, or we shall lose all beauty of form." On the other hand we remember, hardly with surprise, that Dean Inge has contributed his share to the advance of civilisation—not without due recognition, we may hope: "I cannot be too grateful for the generosity of the *Evening Standard*, . . ." as he says in *More Lay Thoughts of a Dean*. He has asserted authority in multifarious provinces, and maintained standards, particularly in the matter of Christian gentility: "He was no gentleman," he says of Donne, "and a very equivocal Christian. I have a rooted distrust of men of letters who, like Donne, Huysmans, and the African novelist, Apuleius, wallow in garbage for many years, and then suddenly 'get religion.'"

To-day journalism solicits us everywhere, and the academic conception of tradition, clearly, does not save its champions from wallowing. There are, of course in the Royal Society of Literature more respectable representatives of the academic mind than Dean Inge, and the aristocratic tradition is also represented. So, since we are also told that is is the policy of the Society "to focus its prestige" by "adding to itself under a rigorous system of election a majority of the most distinguished writers of the time," we can still be interested. We look anxiously to see who these writers are. Mr. Laurence Binyon is one, we must suppose. Mr. de la Mare is also of the Society. However, he cancels out against Mr. John Drinkwater, who is also there: any "recognised authority" hoping to impose on us "a high standard in matters of intellect and taste" must combat the confusion that lumps Mr. de la Mare and Mr. Drinkwater together as "Georgian poets." Mr. G. K. Chesterton is also a member, which, perhaps, may pass without comment one way or the other. But when we come to Mr. Hugh Walpole and Miss Clemence Dane we know that the worst is true and the hope was foolish. For Mr. Walpole and Miss Dane are two-fifths of the Book Society Ltd. (or, to be strict, of the Selection Committee) and Miss Dane wrote a book on "the traditive novel" called *Tradition and Hugh Walpole.*

There are other Fellows. There is Miss V. Sackville West, for instance, who, addressing the Society on *Some Tendencies of Modern English Poetry* (1927) contends that "free verse" is a "more civilised form" than the other kinds. But this can hardly tend to make Mr. Eliot feel more at home in the Society (for we find him to our astonishment a Fellow).

Nor can his presence in such company tend to reverse our conclusion as to the influence of the Society on standards.

The Royal Society of Literature, we must conclude, has no function, unless the incidental one of hall-marking the kind of literature standardised by the Book Society, Ltd.

The English Association, which in our search for a likely organ we turn to next, can, on the other hand make out a very strong case for its existence. Its province is education, and its function, in brief, to organise throughout the country such interest in English literature as will admit of organisation. But in the absence of any serious current standards or any "central authority representing higher culture and sound judgment," what can it do, we ask, to supply the lack, or to resist the triumphant enemy? And we note with misgiving in the Bulletins of the Association the prominence of certain familiar names, the interlocking with the Royal Society of Literature. But we are not in a hurry to generalise, or to cast up the account, though we get many disquieting glimpses both of the educational work in the country at large and of proceedings at the top of the hierarchy. What Mr. Alfred Noyes is reported as saying to various branches might be adapted and applied to lectures and addresses sponsored by the Association: "It was perfectly obvious, he said, that many people who wrote about poetry didn't know what they were writing about." There are lectures on Mr. Walpole's and Mr. Priestley's novels, and even on Mr. Priestley's schooldays. And the healthy-minded dislike of intelligence voiced by Colonel John Buchan does come to have the effect of a corporate spirit: "Again," he says, championing the Victorians in an address called *The Novel and the Fairy Tale* (July, 1931), "they were not clever people, like those who decry them, and in this they were akin to the ordinary man, who is nearly as suspicious of mere cleverness as Mr. Baldwin." Still, some compromise, perhaps, there must be, and if culture is to enjoy the support of Good-Fellowship it must pay the price; the Good-Fellow ticket is inevitably the anti-highbrow.

But after a glance through the current Bulletin (December, 1931) one's suspicion that the price may leave nothing worth keeping becomes something more than a suspicion. For Professor Oliver Elton, elected President for 1932, speaking at the Annual Dinner of the Association, with the Archbishop of Canterbury in the chair, is reported as having concluded: "At any rate, whether we are saints or whether we are not saints, we shall all be the better for doing two things, reading the novels of Mr. Hugh Walpole and being members and supporters of the English Association." Dr. Elton was not speaking without precedent: the *entente* between the English Association and the Book Society had already been well advertised. At the Annual Dinner a year before, Mr. Hugh Walpole, Chairman of Committee (succeeding Mr. J. C. Squire), had said with reference to Mr. J. B. Priestley (once of the

Book Society) "This is the point that I wish to make; that he has, particularly by a recent book of his which we all know, given a new dignity to the position of the 'best seller.' It is, I believe, a best seller, and it deserves to be. To call it a classic would be, of course, premature and perhaps exaggerated, but I think to say that it is a work of very high literary excellence and that it will live is not going too far." Mr. Priestley, unfortunately, wasn't present to make the graceful reply, but the President of Magdalen, another fifth of the Selection Committee of the Book Society, Ltd., was, so that Mr. Walpole's "eminence in letters and enthusiasm for literature" did not go unsignalised.

Is it necessary to inquire further? Looking over the reports of educational work in the country generally we can no longer doubt that it is largely a matter of propagating, and endorsing with the authority and prestige of the Association, the standards of the Book Society. If anyone still hesitates to concur, there is the field of poetry to consider, where, unhappily, we are left no excuse for suspending judgment. For the English Association is responsible for the anthology, very widely used in schools, called *Poems of To-day*, the two volumes of which (as I have heard indignant teachers who have to use it lament) contain between them hardly half-a-dozen good poems. The importance of *Poems of To-day* to the finances of the Association is referred to at most Annual General Meetings. At the Annual Dinner, 1926, Mr. Baldwin, as

President-elect, said: "We are solvent, we are considerably on the right side; but that is because we have been living on the earnings of *Poems of To-day*. We hope to follow it up with equally profitable publications."—A concise statement of the position: there can be no pleasure in dwelling on the irony.

The worst suspicions aroused by the Royal Society of Literature, then, have been confirmed. There is nothing for it but to conclude that, in the absence of current standards maintained by the authority of tradition, official machinery can only gear in with the mechanism of standardisation and levelling-down—can, at the best, only endorse Book Society values. The L.N.E.R. advertises that it "brings you to Priestley's England." The English Association is helping to bring us all to the Book Society's England.

It is then, without extravagant hopes that we turn to the British Broadcasting Corporation, the new organ of culture of which so much is expected. It has been taking its function with admirable seriousness. Last winter's set of talks entitled *This Changing World* was a laudable attempt at educating the public to cope with the modern environment. And good educational work the B.B.C. has, in some sense, undoubtedly done. But how little it can be expected to reverse the process we have been contemplating, to educate in the sense of promulgating standards that would make the Walpole-Priestley *régime* appear what it is, Mr. Harold

Nicolson's notorious talks on *The New Spirit in Literature* should have been sufficient to establish.

Mr. Nicolson's talks were notorious because of the disapproving comment they provoked, and its sequel. They were not notorious for their extravagant absurdity, their vulgarity and their sciolism; the objectors did not point out that Mr. Nicolson had obviously not the first qualification for the undertaking upon which he had embarked with such assurance. However, it might be urged that the mere undertaking was something; it was at least a challenge to Book Society values. That it was so Mr. Nicolson took pains to deny, and we have here the most significant aspect of the whole affair.

"I have," he assured his listeners, "a great respect for Mr. Hugh Walpole, who in more than one way has rendered valuable service to literature."—(Mr. Nicolson was perhaps thinking of the Book Society and the English Association.)—"I admire his character and I have often admired his books." The assurance was as explicit as possible. "I have no doubt whatsoever regarding the literary integrity of Mr. Walpole and Mr. Priestley. And I like their smiles. I might even go further. I might admit that writers such as these two stand in a more direct relation to the continuity of British letters than do any of the authors whom I shall discuss in this series. I am perfectly prepared to believe that they represent a 'better' school of writing than do my own poor neurotics."—(*Listener*, November, 4, 1931).

So it is not, all things considered, surprising that Mr. Nicolson should go on to ask: "What, then, is the gulf that separates Mr. Walpole and me in literary matters?"

What indeed? And we might still have asked, even if Mr. Nicolson had re-iterated disagreement instead of agreement. For debate at Mr. Walpole's level could have no place in a serious discussion of modern literature, and there could be no serious discussion of modern literature that should not be an implicit condemnation of Mr. Walpole and Mr. Priestley. Mr. Nicolson, in fact, even if he had been qualified to explain Mr. Eliot and Mr. Joyce and Mrs. Woolf, would have been better employed explaining how Mr. Walpole and Mr. Priestley are, "in more than one way," *not* rendering valuable services to literature.

This, of course, he could not have been allowed to do had he so desired. And that is really the final comment on the kind of undertaking he took part in. A serious experiment in cultural education would have to start by doing what is and must remain forbidden. There *are* authorities that may not be challenged, but none of the kind we are looking for. And there can be none.

As for Mr. Nicolson's embarrassing performance over the wireless, we should remind ourselves that he wrote in *Some People* a book of a certain distinction and that his *Tennyson* and his *Swinburne* are not negligible. These books are the work of a cultivated man of some talent, and his case is the more interesting and the more illustrative of the times. These are the times in which the acquiring of taste and discrimination and "sensitiveness of intelligence," is probably harder than ever before in the history of civilisation. The *Listener*, in which Mr. Nicolson's talks were printed, reminds us—none the less for the good quality of much of its contents—of his real excuse. In the environment it represents, the tropical profusion of topics and vocabularies and the absence of a cultural grammar and syntax, what chance had he? Such an environment does not favour "sensitiveness of intelligence," which, as Arnold tells us, produces "deference to a standard higher than one's own habitual standard." And where is such a standard to be found? So a man may discuss "matters of taste and intellect" with the best people, and never be troubled even by the ghost of authority. And, now himself authority, so far from being able to induce "sensitiveness of intelligence" in his listeners, he is himself demoralised and can tell them seriously that the "modernists" (conforming to progressive evolution, and interpreting man's unconquerable mind) preach: "Sex is a form of food; do not starve it, yet do not guzzle" (*Listener*, November, 25).

With no standards above, inherent in a living tradition that gives them authority, education can be only a matter of so much more machinery, geared to the general machine of civilisation. I could produce the familiar evidence from the field of democratic adult education (lectures on Walpole and Priestley, etc.), but there has been much devoted work, and here, in any case, I would rather not risk being thought to take pleasure in irony.

Standards above, invested with effective authority —were there ever any? Were things ever much different? That such questions can be asked (as they commonly are) brings home the completeness of the change. There is no room here even to hint at the kind of evidence that can be marshalled. I can only reply that before the last century, in, say, Johnson's time, it never occurred to anyone to question that there were, in all things, standards above the level of the ordinary man. That this was so, and the advantage the ordinary man derived, might be brought home by a study (one is in fact being written) of the memoirs and autobiographies, which exist in considerable numbers of persons of the humblest origin who raised themselves to intellectual distinction and culture. Johnson's own appeal to the "common reader," which is sometimes invoked in support of the democratic principle in criticism, has (odd that I should have to say it!) an opposite force. It testifies how far Johnson was from suspecting that there could ever be a state of affairs like that existing now. He could rejoice to concur with the "common reader" because taste was then in the keeping of the educated who, sharing a homogeneous culture, maintained in tradition a surer taste than any that is merely individual can be, and he could not have imagined such an authority being seriously challenged. To-day, as the Editors of *Scrutiny* pointed out in their first editorial, there is no such common reader.

And yet there are some to whom the substance of this essay is commonplace, otherwise it would not have been worth writing: where there are some to whom it is commonplace there are some to whom the commonplace has not come home in all its force. This is to suggest that full recognition from those capable of it is worth striving for; and that implies more. It is certainly not to suggest any simple prescription. For if what Matthew Arnold, pondering the Literary Influence of Academies, said seventy years ago might still be said, it would be with a very different accent:

> "It is not that there do not exist in England, as in France, a number of people perfectly well able to discern what is good, in these things, from what is bad; but they are isolated, they form no powerful body of opinion, they are not strong enough to set a standard. . . . Ignorance and charlatanism . . . are always trying to pass off their wares as excellent, and to cry down criticism as the voice of an insignificant, over-fastidious minority; they easily persuade the multitude that this is so when the minority is scattered about as it is here. . . ."

1932.

BABBITT BUYS THE WORLD[1]

"*Mental democracy and machine organisation triumph, and in the process, Babbitt buys the world.*"
—E. A. Mowrer, *This American World.*

"FEW people" notes Mr. Wells on p. 199, "can be trusted to cut and arrange their own toe-nails well." He is describing, with the detail that this extract suggests, the particular advance of civilisation represented by the beautician's parlour. "Museums are littered with the rouge cups, trays, manicure sets, mirrors and pots for greases and messes, of the pretty ladies of Sumeria, Egypt and Babylonia, and thence right down to our own times; but never can the organisation of human adornment have reached the immensity and subtlety shown by these American figures." No, there may be archness, but there is no irony in Mr. Wells's account of the up-to-date ritual. "But, you will say, this is a very exceptional woman, and indeed this is a superfluous section to insert in a survey of world economics!" Wrong! Before long, Mr. Wells implies, many more hundreds of millions a year will be spent on these things, and in a Utopia not very remote (if we will listen to Mr. Wells) *every* woman will enjoy the advantages of rouging, face-lifting, massage, pedicure, manicure, greases and messes even more scientific. This fairly represents the

[1] *The Work, Wealth and Happiness of Mankind*, H. G. Wells.

essential triviality of a large part of *The Work, Wealth and Happiness of Mankind.*

And yet Mr. Well's directing idea—"the re-orientation of loyalties through a realisation of the essential unity of our species"—is not trivial. To this he has devoted his life with a noble disinterestedness. So I reminded myself when, having first thought of declining the task on the ground that Mr. Wells is, at this date, not worth reviewing, I started on this his latest book. We may find it hard to like or respect him, but he is doing work that needs doing and that at the moment seems terribly urgent. Yet we must also remind ourselves that the more his kind of influence seems likely to prevail (and the process of civilisation works with it) the more urgent is drastic criticism. If he belongs to the past it is only in the sense that it has long been impossible to discuss him seriously except as a case, a type, a portent. As such, he matters. More and more the disinterested power in the world seems likely to be Wellsian. Mr. J. M. Keynes hailed *The World of William Clissold* as a distinguished and important book. So the essential points are perhaps worth making once again.

Mr. Wells energises tirelessly on behalf of a "world-machine, planned and efficient, protecting and expanding human life. . . ." And, if there is not a speedy approximation to such a machine the un-Wellsian preoccupations of some of us will, it is plain, soon cease to trouble us or the world. But once the machine is smoothly running, what then?

What is this "expanding," this "richer," life, what are these infinite "possibilities," that Mr. Wells promises us, or rather, the species? Roger Bacon knew (according to Mr. Wells) that if men would listen to him, "Vision and power would reward them. Steamship, aeroplane and automobile, he saw them all, and many other things." Steamship, aeroplane and automobile, and many other things, have already rewarded us. Does "expanding life" mean more and more "vision and power" of this kind? Mr. Wells notoriously thinks it the duty of the civilised man to own or use the latest products of civilisation, and I knew a French friend of his who thought this sense of duty vulgar. But it is plain that what Mr. Wells says of Edison might be adapted to himself: to him "the delights offered by the luxury trades must have seemed extraordinarily stupid." He has found fulfilment in his life's work. He can find his Utopia satisfactory because he has found his actual life satisfactory.

But there are some of us to whom the satisfactions of Edison and Mr. Wells, when offered as ultimate ends, seem insufficient. And Mr. Wells is not unaware of this perversity of human nature. He even devotes the twelfth, and last, volume of his ideal *World Encyclopædia* to "beauty." "In it aesthetic criticism would pursue its wild, incalculable, unstandardised career, mystically distributing praise and blame. . . . The artist in his studio, the composer in his music room and all the multitude who invent and write down their inventions, have hardly figured in our world panorama, and even now we can give them but a passing sentence or two. They are an efflorescence, a lovely and purifying efflorescence on life." In this essay on the "Happiness of Mankind," we can give them but a passing sentence or two. Mr. Wells, of course, believes that if we look after the machinery, they will look after themselves. But the perverse among us persist in urging that looking after the machinery should mean seeing that it works to desired ends, and that a world that gives no more attention to the "lovely efflorescence" than Mr. Wells does is likely not to know what it desires; the efficiency of the machinery becomes the ultimate value, and this seems to us to mean something very different from expanding and richer human life.

Mr. Wells, however, is not interested in this kind of question. And it is for this reason that his book, for all its wealth of information, has a total effect of triviality: the energy that made it seem to the author worth writing is indistinguishable from a schoolboy immaturity of mind. Mr. Wells is praised for his interest in the world, but he is not interested enough. "The story of New Zealand is particularly illuminating," he notes. It is: I know someone who is enquiring why New Zealand has developed nothing in the nature of a distinctive literature. But Mr. Wells's notion of an educated man is one to whom such questions wouldn't be worth troubling about.

Yet inadvertently (he is not an athletic thinker)

he admits their importance—and unwittingly passes judgment on himself. "One peculiar value of the 'Five Towns' novels of Mr. Arnold Bennett lies in the clear, convincing, intimate, and yet almost unpremeditated way in which he shows the industrialised peasant mentality of the employing class in a typical industrialised region, The Black Country, waking up to art and refinement, to ampler personality and new ideas"—The Wellsian man *will* wake up to "art" and "refinement" and "ampler personality" and it will be in Mr. Arnold Bennett's way—a way that, we know, ended in the Imperial Palace Hotel. In spite of Edison's asceticism the inventor, the researcher, the man who gets things done, will seek his guerdon of the "luxury trades." And perhaps even Mr. Wells does not find his work and his Vision quite self-sufficing. Perhaps his interest in beauty-culture is significant. And it is perhaps permissible to suggest that specialised sexual charm counts for more in his scheme of things than a mature mind could think worthy; Mr. Wells will not blush.

But he might, perhaps, blush if one pointed out the falsities of his book in matters of fact. Take, for instance, his naïve account of beauticianry: he pays here, as the articles on the Beauty Racket published recently in the *New Republic* might bring home to him, involuntary tribute to the power of advertising that he acclaims elsewhere. Again, he has swallowed with completely uncritical innocence the official Ford legend. Let him read *The Tragedy of Henry Ford* by Jonathan Norton Leonard. This book is just out, but so much was already common knowledge that Mr. Wells cannot be acquitted of complicity—he was not an unwilling gull. This may seem a severe verdict. But read him on the "ultra-scholastic education" that the "citizen" gets from newspapers, radio, cinema, and so on (pp. 745 ff.): "On the whole, it is sound stuff he gets." I know that Mr. Well's criteria are not mine; but even by his own what he lets out elsewhere is enough to brand his complacency as something worse.

We can respect him as we cannot respect Arnold Bennett, but it is significant that, for all his disinterestedness, he is not safe from the Arnold Bennett corruption.

1932.

ARNOLD BENNETT: AMERICAN VERSION[1]

THIS book is a document of unusual interest. That is not to pronounce it a good book. Indeed, its badness is an essential part of its documentary value, and is the reason, it might be said, for recommending it. "It is a historical study of a phase of culture" (according to the dust-cover); it is a "Novel of Facts" (according to the author); and it is, unintentionally, a fascinating document of cultural dissolution. An intelligent account of Dreiser's career might have been very interesting, but it could hardly have been so convincing or have told us more.

Dreiser, I have heard it remarked, shows us what there is to be said for Arnold Bennett. And the tropical rankness and profusion of the American phenomenon do indeed make the English analogue look chaste and austere—by comparison a triumph of spirit rather than of philistinism. The Man from the Middle West also made good in women's journalism, and on a much larger scale than the Man from the North: "As five-fold Butterick editor and art-editor, he came as near to big business as any periodical in that day could bring him. He had a staff of thirty-two people." His friends might

[1] *Dreiser and the Land of the Free*, Dorothy Dudley.

laugh "to think of him in this low-brow guise of fashion-dictator, but with characteristic seriousness and without shame he studied the problem—how to reach the ladies. He stimulated with ideas; ideas gave birth to longings, and longings to the need of new clothes. Women over the country felt that somehow a friend of theirs was breathing a tiny wind of danger into Butterick standards." Before this he had had a shining career in newspapers and in a publishing firm of which the motto was: "The worse the swill the better you can sell it."

All this, and a great deal more, the rich extravagance of which cannot be even faintly suggested, Miss Dudley relates with complete and solemn complaisance: it is Dreiser "carving a destiny." True, her central preoccupation is his conquest of recognition as a writer. But she does not convey any sense of there being essential differences between his various activities—they all manifest his greatness. In short, she is as completely in and of her material, as completely innocent of values by which it might be even implicitly criticised, as Dreiser is with regard to his own novels.

This innocence, illustrated fantastically and almost incredibly throughout the book, constitutes its great significance. The author supposes her main theme to be the hostility in Dreiser's time of the American environment towards the artist. If she establishes it, it is not in the way she intends—though "intention," suggesting as it does something simple and clear, is perhaps misleading: the book is essentially a matter of getting it both or, if possible, more ways. Dreiser the lonely rebel, for instance, is explicitly and triumphantly represented as the incarnation of the spirit that has made modern America—the passion for "supremacy," no matter of what kind so long as it means recognition and "luxury and refinement" (i.e. the American equivalents of Bennett's steam-yacht and Imperial Palace Hotel).

The only serious show of a case for making out hostility in this congenial environment is that Drieser's novels fell foul of the lagging Victorian prudery of America. He did have genuine grievances against timid publishers, moral reviewers and comstockery in general. And it does seem that, as a matter of history, his was the decisive challenge: an American writer may now put as much of "life" into his novel as he likes. But it does not follow that Dreiser is a great writer, or in any respect an innovator in his art. Miss Dudley repeats again and again, with ironical intention, the charge that he cannot write and has no feeling for words, but she does not refute it. Everything of his she quotes confirms it: his mode of expression is what one would expect of the school in which he learnt. And it isn't merely mode of expression, it is quality of mind: *Sister Carrie* is full of stuff that reminds one comically of *Tarzan of the Apes.* As for his method and approach, they are Edwardian: it is significant that H. G. Wells, Arnold Bennett and W. J. Locke were among the first to recognise him. It is perhaps also significant (or would be, if she were a little less completely without critical perception) that Miss Dudley, who pours out the names of American writers, incontinently and indiscriminately, as current coin, hardly mentions John Dos Passos (though her own enterprise suggests his influence).

The name of Dos Passos is at any rate, relevant here. *Manhattan Transfer, Forty-second Parallel* and *Nineteen-nineteen*, not only represent a standard that makes Miss Dudley's claim for Dreiser look silly; they leave no excuse for supposing that an antiquated moral code was the chief cause of sterility and that its dissolution means that all will now go well. But there is every reason to suppose that Miss Dudley would not see the meaning of these truly remarkable works of literature. She quotes Pascin as saying, "It takes twice as much genius to paint in America as it does in France," but she clearly doesn't understand.

The artist in America, she complains, has been barred out of Society. The disadvantage?—

"Take another example, D. H. Lawrence, son of a coal miner, as Dreiser was son of a foreman in a woollen mill, and Sandburg of a blacksmith, and Anderson of a house painter. In *Lady Chatterley's Lover* sex seems awkward, even inexperienced, but English manners are authentic enough to create the illusion of society. And why? Because Lawrence found himself dragged into drawing rooms, whether he liked it or not. . . ."

That's what snobbery (there was Mrs. John Jacob

Astor, for instance) denied the American artist. But this need to know upper-class manners appears for the most part indistinguishable from the need for "luxury," the need to master "the art of enjoyment." This art is interpreted in a way that makes the heading of this review excessively unfair to Arnold Bennett.

No one who has not read the book can imagine the tone in which the hero's very ordinary and very ugly sexual promiscuity is exhibited—"this trait which forced selection and action." Genius, it appears, needs the ideal woman. The ideal woman is hard to find—one after another the experiments turn out disappointing. But Dreiser has, at any rate, decided that eighteen is the right age, and nowadays generally picks on that.

Miss Dudley's book, then, deserves to be called classical for the completeness with which it presents its case, and should be read by all who wish to be clear why Western civilisation seems less and less likely to favour art and literature.

JOHN DOS PASSOS[1]

AFTER *Manhattan Transfer* (1927) one remembered the name of John Dos Passos. After *The Forty-second Parallel* one looked eagerly forward to the succeeding members of the trilogy (for something of that order seemed to be promised) in the conviction that we had here a work demanding serious attention as no other appearing under the head of the novel during the past two or three years had done. *Nineteen-nineteen* is a challenge to justify the conviction.

The Forty-second Parallel established Mr. Dos Passos as an unusually serious artist—serious with the seriousness that expresses itself in the propagandist spirit. Unlike Mrs. Woolf, his antithesis, he cannot be interested in individuals without consciously relating them to the society and the civilisation that make the individual life possible. Consequently, society and civilisation being to-day what they are, his stress falls elsewhere than upon the individual life as such. In *Manhattan Transfer* his theme is New York, representing our "megalopolitan" civilisation: "The terrible thing about having New York go stale on you is that there's nowhere else. It's the top of the world. All we can do is to go round and round in a squirrel's cage."

[1] *Manhattan Transfer; The Forty-second Parallel; Nineteen-nineteen.*

The undertaking involves a peculiar technical problem, one that none of the methods customarily associated with the novel will meet. No amount of enthusiasm for collective humanity will dispose of the fact that it is only in individuals that humanity lives, that only in the individual focus does consciousness function, that only individuals enjoy and suffer; and the problem is to suggest that multitudinous impersonality of the ant-heap through individual cases that, without much development, interest us as such. *Manhattan Transfer* represents a sufficient degree of success. It is of the essence of Mr. Dos Passos' method here—and of his vision of modern life—that of no one of his swirl of "cases" do we feel that it might profitably be developed into a separate novel; and yet we are interested enough. Here we have them in poignant individuality, a representative assortment of average men and women, engaged in the "pursuit of happiness"—a pursuit sanctioned by the Constitution, but, of its very nature, and by the very conditions of the civilisation to which they belong, vain. "'Darling, I'm so happy. . . . It's really going to be worth living now.'" Money, Success, Security, Love—in varied and ironical iteration we see the confident clutch: 'Elaine,' he said shakily, 'life's really going to mean something to me now . . . God, if you knew how empty life had been for so many years. I've been like a tin mechanical toy, all hollow inside.'"

Manhattan Transfer ends with Jimmy Herf (the

character to whom the author seems closest) walking, with an air of symbolic finality, out of New York. *The Forty-second Parallel* gives us the America into which he walks—a large undertaking, which calls for some modification of technique. The representative lives stand out more and are given less in episode-dialogue and more in consecutive narrative; narrative admirably managed in *tempo*, and varied dramatically in idiom with the chief actor. The "News-reels" interspersed at intervals are a new device, their function being by means of newspaper-clippings and the like, in ironical medley, to establish the background of the contemporary public world. Moreover, also at intervals, there are lives, admirably compressed and stylised in what might be called prose-poems, of the makers, the heroes, the great men, the public figures, of American civilisation. Thus Mr. Dos Passos seeks to provide something corresponding to the symbolic figures of a national epic or saga.

In general, for him, to be representative is to be unimpressive, and of his private characters only one is impressive and saga-like in his representativeness: J. Ward Moorhouse, "public relations counsel." It is significant. In him is embodied the power that, in the general disintegration, in the default of religion, art and traditional forms and sanctions, holds society together—the Power of the Word, or, let us say, Advertising. "Clean cut young executive," says J. Ward Moorhouse, looking at himself in the glass: the magician has reason to believe in the magic; it works for him. On this theme the author's art achieves some of its triumphs, and the aspect of modern civilisation it exhibits is terrifying. "We are handling this matter from the human interest angle . . . pity and tears, you understand"—can a hundred D. H. Lawrences preserve even the idea of emotional sincerity against the unremitting, pervasive, masturbatory manipulations of "scientific" Publicity, and, what is the same thing, commercially supplied popular art?

"In America a fellow can get ahead. Birth don't matter, education don't matter. It's all getting ahead." In the close of *The Forty-second Parallel* we see America welcoming an escape from this "getting ahead," a "meaning" with which to exorcise the void, in the War. *Nineteen-nineteen* gives us the War. The second part of the trilogy is decidedly less lively than the first. For one thing, the monotony of this world without religion, morality art or culture is here, perhaps inevitably, emphasised. And this leads us to the more general question: What is lacking in the work as a whole (so far as we have it)?—why, in spite of its complete and rare seriousness, does it fall so decidedly short of being great?

For answer we have the state of civilisation it celebrates. "I guess all he needs is to go to work and get a sense of values," says a character in *Manhattan Transfer*, exemplifying one of the author's best ironic effects. The comment on the prescription is the society portrayed: what kind of a sense of values can one acquire, what does a sense of values mean, in such an environment? The artistic shortcomings of Mr. Dos Passos' most ambitious work (which is not, like *Manhattan Transfer*, held together by the topographical limits of the setting) might thus be, not merely excused as inevitable, but extolled as propagandist virtues: they are necessary to a work that exhibits the decay of capitalistic society.

The argument, of course, would be specious. And the point in view might be made most effectively by reframing the question to run: What is lacking in the work as propaganda? This question is answered by asking what it is that Mr. Dos Passos offers us in the way of hope. The suggestion of hope, if it is one, that *Nineteen-nineteen* ends upon is revolution. Whether Mr. Dos Passos intends irony will, perhaps, be made plain in the last volume of the trilogy; but, as it is, the promise must appear as ironical as that upon which *The Forty-second Parallel* closed. Someone in *Nineteen-nineteen* says: "it will take some huge wave of hope like a revolution to make me feel any self-respect ever again." Such a wave of hope, in a world inhabited by Mr. Dos Passos' characters, would, it must seem, be of much the same order as the wave engendered by the outbreak of the War. His revolutionaries are as inadequate, as much "tin mechanical toys, all hollow inside," as his other persons. He plainly realises this where they are intellectuals; where they are proletarians there is something embarrassingly like sentimentality in his attitude.

It may be that the concluding volume of the trilogy will show this last comment to be unfair in its implications. And perhaps comment on the inadequacy of individuals is discounted by Mr. Dos Passos' philosophy. Nevertheless a literary critic must venture the further judgment that the shortcomings of the work both as art and propaganda are related to a certain insufficiency in it when it is considered as an expression of personality (which on any theory a work of art must in some sense be). It is more than a superficial analogy when the technique is likened to that of the film. The author might be said to conceive his function as selective photography and "montage." That this method does not admit sufficiently of the presence of the artist's personal consciousness the device called "The Camera Eye" seems to recognise—it at any rate seems to do little else. What this judgment amounts to is that the work does not express an adequate realisation of the issues it offers to deal with.

How far the defect is due to the method, and how far it lies in the consciousness behind the method, one cannot presume to determine. But Mr. Dos Passos, though he exhibits so overwhelmingly the results of disintegration and decay, shows nothing like an adequate awareness of—or concern for—what has been lost. Perhaps we have here the disability corresponding to the advantage he enjoys as an American. In America the Western process has gone furthest, and what has been lost is virtually forgotten. Certainly Mr. Dos Passos seems to share

—it is a confirming sign—the attitude towards art and literature that so curiously qualifies the intelligence and penetration of Mr. Edmund Wilson's *Axel's Castle* (a book which only an American could have written). "Art," for the aspirant to "culture" in *The Forty-second Parallel,* is "something ivory-white and very pure and noble and distant and sad." The mind behind "The Camera Eye" seems to conceive of "culture" after much the same fashion in rejecting it: ". . . grow cold with culture like a cup of tea forgotten between an incense burner and a volume of Oscar Wilde."

What has disintegrated—this is the point—is not merely "bourgeois" or "capitalist" civilisation; it is the organic community. Instead of the rural community and the town community we have, almost universally, suburbanism (for the nature and significance of suburbanism see the article by Mr. W. L. Cuttle in *The Universities Review* for October, 1931). The organic community has virtually disappeared, and with it the basis for a genuine national culture; so nearly disappeared that when one speaks of the old popular culture that existed in innumerable local variations people cannot grasp what one means. This is no place to try and explain. But let them re-read *The Pilgrim's Progress* and consider its significance, *Change in the Village, The Wheelwright's Shop*, and the other works of George Bourne, and, say, Cecil Torr's *Small Talk at Wreyland*, and then, for a commentary on the passing of the old order, go to *Middletown.* The education in reading offered, for instance, under the auspices of the W.E.A., is a substitute, and, as everyone who has lent a hand in it must at some time have realised, a substitute that can hardly begin to negotiate with the student's needs, and so must almost inevitably tend to a conception of Art as "something ivory-white and very pure and distant and sad." (It is relevant here to note that Mr. J. H. Fowler, in *The Art of Teaching English*, holds Ruskin to be "the greatest writer of English prose that ever lived.")

The memory of the old order, the old ways of life, must be the chief hint for, the directing incitement towards, a new, if ever there is to be a new. It is the memory of a human normality or naturalness (one may recognise it as such without ignoring what has been gained in hygiene, public humanity and comfort). Whether, in a world of continually developing machine technique, a new order will ever be able to grow may seem doubtful. But without the faith that one might be achieved there can hardly be hope in revolution. "There'd be gaiety for the workers then, after the revolution," says someone in *Manhattan Transfer*. And in *The Forty-second Parallel* we read of "quiet men who wanted a house with a porch to putter around, and a fat wife to cook for them, a few drinks and cigars, and a garden to dig in." This is all that Mr. Dos Passos suggests (as yet) concerning the way in which meaning is to be restored to the agonised vacuity that it is his distinction to convey so potently.

It seems to me the more one sympathises with his

propagandist intention, the more should one be concerned to stress what is lacking in his presentment of it. To hope that, if the mechanics of civilisation (so to speak) are perfected, the other problems (those which Mr. Dos Passos is mainly preoccupied with) will solve themselves, is vain: "you know," says someone in *Nineteen-nineteen*, "the kind of feeling when everything you've wanted crumbles in your fingers as you grasp it." Men and women might, of course, find happiness—or release from unhappiness—as perfect accessory machines. But that is hardly a hope for a propagandist to offer.

1932.

D. H. LAWRENCE

TO write critically on D. H. Lawrence is a rash undertaking. There have been many warnings. Eminent critics have shown by example how difficult and perilous it is. To make Lawrence an occasion for asserting one's superiority over Bouvard and Pécuchet, Babbitt and Viscount Brentford is easy, but it is hard to be critical without getting oneself confused with his subtly malicious depreciators.

I start, then, by assuming that "genius" is the right word for Lawrence, though, in a recent "affair," an incomparably better critic than myself did this, and it did not save him from rebuke. Perhaps the ascription has been too long a commonplace. "In the early days," says Lawrence, in an *Autobiographical Sketch* reprinted in *Assorted Articles*, "they were always telling me I had got genius, as if to console me for not having their own incomparable advantages." So I had better say at once what I mean by ascribing genius to Lawrence. I have in mind the same kind of thing as when I say that Blake obviously had genius. Lawrence had it as obviously. He had the same gift of knowing, what he was interested in, the same power of distinguishing his own feelings and emotions from conventional sentiment, the same "terrifying honesty." Blake's name suggests itself so readily for this comparison because there is between him and Lawrence a significant parallel which might be worked out in some detail. It will be enough here to quote a few Laurentian passages:

"It is wrong to make the lion lie down with the lamb. This is the supreme sin, the unforgivable blasphemy of which Christ spoke. This is the creation of nothingness, the bringing about, or the striving to bring about the nihil which is pure meaninglessness."[1]

"But it is the fight of opposites which is holy. The fight of like things is evil."[2]

"In the seed of the dandelion, as it floats in its little umbrella of hairs, sits the Holy Ghost in tiny compass."[3]

"So the tiger, striped in gold and black, lies and stretches his limbs in perfection between all that the day is, and all that is night. . . . When he stretches himself superbly, he stretches himself between the living day, and the living night, the vast inexhaustible duality of creation. And he is the fanged and brindled Holy Ghost, with ice-shining whiskers."[4]

"The sun, I tell you, is alive, and more alive than I am, or a tree is. It may have blazing gas, as I have hair, as a tree has leaves. But I tell you, it is the Holy Ghost in full raiment, shaking and walking, alive as a tiger is, only more so."[5]

Passing from prophecy to squibs, one might point to *Pansies* and *Nettles*, which remind one of the similar verse in which Blake sought relief.

[1] *The Crown.* [2] *Ibid.*

[3] *Reflections on the Death of a Porcupine.* [4] *Aristocracy.*

[5] *Ibid.*

"'What?' it will be questioned. 'When the sun rises do you not see a round disk of fire something like a guinea?' Oh! No! no! I see an innumerable company of the heavenly host crying 'Holy, holy, holy, is the Lord God Almighty!'" Blake: note on *The Last Judgment.*

The community between Blake's and Lawrence's preoccupations is obvious: they might both be said to have been concerned with the vindication of impulse and spontaneity against "reason" and convention. The difference between them is the more interesting in that it is more than the difference between individuals. In the background of Blake are Rousseau and the French Revolution. In the background of Lawrence are the social transformations of the nineteenth century, Darwin, Dostoevsky, Bergson, the War, and an age of psycho-analysis and anthropology. So his search for an inner reality, for the hidden springs of life, took Lawrence a good deal further:

"He turned away. Either the heart would break, or cease to care. Whatever the mystery which has brought forth the universe, it is a non-human mystery, it has its own great ends, man is not the criterion. Best leave it all to the vast, creative non-human mystery. . . . The eternal creative mystery could dispose of man, and replace him with a finer created being. Just as the horse has taken the place of the mastodon.

"It was very consoling to Birkin to think this. . . . The fountain-head was incorruptible and unsearchable. It had no limits. It could bring forth miracles, create utter new races and new species in its own hour, new forms of consciousness, new forms of body, new units of being. To be man was as nothing to the possibilities of the creative mystery. To have one's pulse beating direct from the mystery, this was perfection, unutterable satisfaction. Human or inhuman mattered nothing."[1]

[1] *Women in Love.*

Blake, if he could have thought this, would not have found it consoling. Birkin, of course, though one of Lawrence's obvious self-dramatisations, is not to be taken as completely representative, but it is fair to make this passage an opportunity for noting that Lawrence's preoccupation with the primitive fosters in him a certain inhumanity: the context gives the judgment the appropriate force.

His originality asserts itself in his earliest books. The short stories of *The Prussian Officer*, and his second novel *The Trespasser* (1912) in particular, have an amazing intensity. They make, indeed, oppressive reading, for they evoke states of helpless, tormented servitude to sensation and emotion: we are smothered in the riot of adolescent experience. There is more fresh air in *The White Peacock* (1912), where we find what are to be characteristic themes, scenes and situations. In *Sons and Lovers* (1913), his third novel, he is mature, in the sense of being completely himself. It is a beautiful and poignant book, showing a sincerity in the record of emotional life such as is possible only to genius. There we find the complexities of human relations—the tangled attractions and repulsions, self-abasements and tyrannies of love in particular—exposed with the fanatical seriousness characteristic of Lawrence. According to Mr. Middleton Murry (in the *New Adelphi* for June–August, 1930) it was quickly discovered "that in *Sons and Lovers* Lawrence had independently arrived at the main conclusions of the psycho-analysts, and the English followers of

Freud came to see him." Besides this psychological subtlety, the book (like *The White Peacock* and all the early work) is remarkable for a sensuous richness of a kind that leads one to talk loosely of the author as a "poet." (He did indeed write verse, but not much of it is poetry, though it is very interesting in various ways: he rarely attained the level of the *Ballad of a Second Ophelia*.) This richness may be seen at its best in the lovely passage at the opening of *The Rainbow*. It derives from his poignant intuition of the common flame in all things that live and grow; from his sense of the mysterious intercourse of man with the world around him:

"But heaven and earth was teeming around them, and how should this cease? They felt the rush of the sap in spring, they knew the wave which cannot halt, but every year throws forward the seed to begetting, and, falling back, leaves the young-born on the earth. They knew the intercourse between heaven and earth, sunshine drawn into the breast and bowels, the rain sucked up in the daytime, nakedness that comes under the wind in autumn, showing the bird's nests no longer worth hiding. Their life and interrelations were such; feeling the pulse and body of the soil, that opened to their furrow for the grain, and became smooth and supple after their ploughing, and clung to their feet with a weight that pulled like desire, lying hard and unresponsive when the crops were to be shorn away. The young corn waved and was silken, and the lustre slid along the limbs of the men who saw it. They took the udder of the cows, the cows yielded milk and pulse against the hands of the men, the pulse of the blood of the teats of the cows beat into the pulse of the hands of the men. They mounted their horses, and held life between the grip of their knees, they harnessed their horses at the wagon, and, with hand on the bridle rings, drew the heaving of the horses after their will.

"In autumn the partridges whirred up, birds in flocks blew like spray across the fallow, rooks appeared on the grey, watery heavens, and flew cawing into the winter. Then the men sat by the fire in the house where the women moved about with surety, and the limbs and the body of the men were impregnated with the day, cattle and earth and vegetation and sky, the men sat by the fire and their brains were inert, as their blood flowed heavy with the accumulation from the living day."

Sons and Lovers bears obviously a close relation to Lawrence's personal history. *The Rainbow*[1] (1915) deals with three generations, yet it seems to bear much the same kind of relation to personal experience. In fact, Lawrence here is exploring his own

[1] "We are the foam and the foreshore, that which, between the two oceans, is not, but which supersedes the oceans in utter reality, and gleams in absolute Eternity.

The Beginning is not, nor the eternity which lies behind us, save in part. Partial also is the eternity which lies in front. But that which is not partial, but whole, that which is not relative, but absolute is the clash of the two into one, the foam of being thrown up into consummation.

It is the music which comes when the cymbals clash one upon the other: this is absolute and timeless. The cymbals swing back in one or the other direction of time, towards one or the other relative eternity. But absolute, timeless, beyond time or eternity, beyond space or infinity, is the music that was the consummation of the two cymbals in opposition.

It is that which comes when night clashes on day, the rainbow, the yellow and rose and blue and purple of dawn and sunset, which leaps out of the breaking light upon darkness, of darkness upon light, absolute beyond day or night; the rainbow, the iridescence, which is darkness at once and light, the two-in-one; the crown that binds them both."—*The Crown.*

problems, living them through in the book. *Sons and Lovers*, for all its poignant beauty, everyone I have discussed it with agrees with me in finding difficult to get through. *The Rainbow* is a great deal more difficult. We do not doubt the urgency for the author of these shifting tensions of the inner life, this drama of the inexplicit and almost inexpressible in human intercourse, but for us the effect is one of monotony. Lawrence's fanatical concern for the "essential" often results in a strange intensity, but how limited is the range! And the intensity too often fails to come through to us. Behind these words we know there are agonies of frustration, deadlock and apprehension, but we only see words. Moreover, paradoxically, the concern to make a prophetic communication about life, a communication that is symbolised by the "rainbow," itself tends to monotony as much as to beauty.

Lawrence is exploring his problems, living them through, in all his novels, but from *The Rainbow* onwards we are aware of certain conclusions. Indeed he insists on our being aware of them, for, not content to leave them implicit, he enforces them by illustration, comment and symbolism. He becomes, in fact, a prophet, and imposes on the critic the same kind of task as Blake does.

> "The amazingly difficult and vital business of human relationship has been almost laughably underestimated in our epoch. All this nonsense about love and unselfishness, more crude and repugnant than savage fetish worship. Love is a thing to be *learned*, through centuries of patient effort. It is a

difficult complex maintenance of individual integrity throughout the incalculable process of interhuman polarity."[1]

This, except perhaps for the last sentence, does not sound too formidable. But Lawrence's conclusions involve also a great deal of declaiming against "ideas," "ideals" and "mind-knowledge." For he arrived at a passionate conviction that man is destroying himself with consciousness, with self-consciousness. The good life, he believed, depends upon complete emotional spontaneity, and this has been made impossible for us by self-consciousness, by "ideals," by "mind-knowledge." ("Blake, too," he says, "was one of these ghastly, obscene 'knowers.'") The aim, then, is to throw off all ideas of how we ought to feel, all will to feel one way rather than another, "so that that which is perfectly ourselves can take place in us."[2] But this summary might be held to be unfair to Lawrence, so I will quote one of his own many accounts:

"The whole field of dynamic and effectual consciousness is *always* pre-mental, non-mental. Not even the most knowing man that ever lived would know how he would be feeling next week; whether some new and utterly shattering impulse would have arisen in him and laid his nicely conceived self in

[1] *Psychoanalysis and the Unconscious*, p. 118.

[2] "Every man must live as far as he can by his own soul's conscience. But not according to any ideal. To submit the conscience to a creed, or an idea or a tradition, or even an impulse, is our ruin."—*Fantasia of the Unconscious*, p. 120.

"It is a great task of the liberators, those who work for ever for the liberation of the free spontaneous psyche, the effective soul."—*Psychoanalysis and the Unconscious*, p. 91.

ruins. It is the impulse we have to live by, not the ideals or the idea. But we have to know ourselves pretty thoroughly before we can break the autonomy of ideals and conventions. The savage in a state of nature is one of the most conventional of creatures. So is a child. Only through fine delicate knowledge can we recognise and release our impulses. Now our whole aim has been to force each individual to a maximum of mental control, and mental consciousness. Our poor little plants of children are put into horrible forcing-beds, called schools, and the young idea is there forced to shoot. It shoots, poor thing, like a potato in a warm cellar. One mass of sickly ideas and ideals. And no shoot, no life. The ideas shoot, hard enough, in our sad offspring, but they shoot at the expense of life itself. Never was such a mistake. Mental consciousness is a purely individual affair. Some men are born to be highly and delicately conscious. But for the vast majority, much mental consciousness is simply a catastrophe, a blight. It just stops their living."[1]

Now it would be unprofitable and out of place to discuss these conclusions unattached and in the abstract. They were Lawrence's, and Lawrence was an artist of genius: that is why they are to be considered. And the manner of consideration they demand he himself indicates:

"This pseudo-philosophy of mine—'pollyanalytics,' as one of my respected critics might say—is deduced from the novels and poems, not the reverse. The novels and poems come unwatched out of one's pen. And the absolute need which one has for some sort of satisfactory mental attitude towards oneself and things in general makes one try to abstract some

[1] *Fantasia of the Unconscious*, p. 60.

definite conclusions from one's experiences as a writer and as a man. The novels and poems are pure passionate experience. These 'pollyanalytics' are inferences made afterwards from the experience."[1]

We are to approach, that is, as literary critics. And the manner of the literary critic's concern with these conclusions Lawrence himself suggests:

"Art speech is the only speech,"

he says in *Studies in Classic American Literature*; and in *Lady Chatterley's Lover*:

"It is the way our sympathy flows and recoils that really determines our lives. And here lies the importance of the novel, properly handled. It can inform the lead into new places the flow of our sympathetic consciousness, and it can lead our sympathy away in recoil from things gone dead. Therefore the novel, properly handled, can reveal the most secret places of life—for it is in the *passional* secret places of life, above all, that the tide of sensitive awareness needs to ebb and flow, cleansing and refreshing."

When, so authorised, we consider as a work of art *Women in Love* (written in 1916), a novel in which the mature conclusions are embodied, our judgment cannot be altogether favourable to them. For *Women in Love* hardly "informs and leads into new places the flow of our sympathetic consciousness." To get through it calls for great determination and a keen diagnostic interest. One of the reasons for the difficulty is indicated by this passage:

"He (i.e. Birkin-Lawrence) was not very much interested any more in personalities and in people—

[1] *Fantasia of the Unconscious*, p. 10.

people were all different, but they were all enclosed nowadays in a definite limitation, he said; there were only about two great ideas, two great streams of activity remaining, with various forms of reaction therefrom. The reactions were all varied in various people, but they followed a few great laws, and intrinsically there was no difference. They acted and reacted involuntarily according to a few great laws, and once the laws, the great principles were known, people were no more mystically interesting. They were all essentially alike, the differences were only variations on a theme. None of them transcended the given terms."

Lawrence's main interest lay much lower than personality,[1] and the characters in *Women in Love* tend to disintegrate into swirls of conflicting impulses and emotions. It is difficult to keep them apart. A more radical criticism still is suggested by this passage from *Studies in Classic American Literature:*

"I always remember meeting the eyes of a gypsy woman, for one moment, in a crowd, in England. She knew, and I knew. What did we know? I was not able to make out. But we knew."

It is this kind of knowledge that Lawrence is pervasively concerned with in *Women in Love:* if it can be conveyed at all it is only by poetic means.

[1] These are characteristic descriptions of intense, "significant" experience:

"Her personal eyes had gone blind."—*The Plumed Serpent*, p. 140.

"There was hardly anything to say to him. And there was no personal intimacy. . . . It was his personal presence which enveloped her. She lived in his aura, and he, she knew, lived in hers, with nothing said, and no personal or spiritual intimacy whatever. A mindless communion of the blood."—*Ibid.*, p. 452-3.

But Lawrence uses for the purpose a specialised vocabulary of terms that he tries to invest with a new potency by endless re-iteration: "dark," "pure," "utter," "inchoate," "disintegrate," "uncreated," "violated," "abstract," "mindless," "lapse out," "loins of darkness," and so on. This method is, to use one of Lawrence's own terms of reprobation, mechanical:

> "'Gerald,' he said, 'I rather hate you.'
> 'I know you do,' said Gerald. 'Why do you?'
> Birkin mused inscrutably for some minutes. 'I should like to know if you are conscious of hating me,' he said at last. 'Do you ever consciously detest me—hate me with mystic hate? There are odd moments when I hate you starrily.'"

A great part of the book gets no nearer to concrete particularity than that. And such methods as the insistent minute description of the colours of clothes are equally mechanical.

Failure of this kind, in a man of Lawrence's genius, would seem to imply serious criticism of his "conclusions." Lawrence himself clearly had misgivings: he tried to settle them by putting them into the mouths of characters:

> "What is it but the last and worst form of intellectualism, this love of yours for passion and the animal instincts?"

and

> "You *don't* trust yourself. You don't fully believe yourself what you are saying. You don't really want this conjunction, otherwise you wouldn't talk so much about it, you'd get it."

But even in *Women in Love* the genius of Lawrence is apparent in passages of description, and passages evoking subtle shades of consciousness, strange stirrings of emotion, intuitions of "unknown modes of being." And it must in fairness be stated that never again does he come near to offering, as here, a parallel to the turgid, cyclonic disasters of Blake's prophetic books. His later novels, as he wanders from country to country—Italy, Sardinia, Australia, Mexico—looking for a new mode of consciousness, exhibit in varying measure the kind of defect indicated above: they are fascinating, exasperating, and difficult to read through—at least, at the risk of being included under Mr. Forster's "highbrows whom he bored"[1] I must confess to having found them so: but they do not demand of the reader the desperate resolution that alone will take him through *Women in Love*. Indeed, the next in order of time, *The Lost Girl* (1920) must be exempted from the charge of being difficult to read through. I am inclined to think that it is his best *novel*. The account of the career of James Houghton, retailer in Manchester goods and romantic artist in affairs, is magnificently Dickensian, except that it has none of the weakness of Dickens and all the strength of Lawrence. There is in it no element of farce or caricature; and

[1] "Now he is dead, and the low-brows whom he scandalised have united with the highbrows whom he bored to ignore his greatness. This cannot be helped; no one who alienates both Mrs. Grundy and Aspasia can hope for a good obituary Press. All that we can do . . . is to say straight out that he was the greatest imaginative novelist of our generation." E. M. FORSTER. Letter to the *Nation and Athenæum*, March 29, 1930.

Lawrence's sardonic humour conduces to tragic dignity as sentimental humour could not. But the main theme of the book is suggested by this passage:

"He, Tommy, could quite understand any woman's wanting to marry him—didn't agree a bit with Effie. But marriage, you know, was so final. And then with this war on: you never knew how things might turn out: a foreigner and all that. And then—you won't mind what I say—? We won't talk about class and that rot. If the man's good enough, he's good enough by himself. But is he your intellectual equal, Nurse? After all, it's a big point. You don't want to marry a man you can't talk to—Cicio's a treat to be with because he's so natural. But it isn't a mental treat—

"Alvina thought of Mrs. Tuke, who complained that Tommy talked music and pseudo-philosophy by the hour when he was wound up. She saw Effie's long, outstretched arm of repudiation and weariness.

"Of course!—another of Mrs. Tuke's exclamations. 'Why not *be* atavistic if you *can* be, and follow at a man's heel just because he's a man. Be like barbarous women, a slave.'"

It is very much the theme of Mr. Forster's first book, *Where Angels fear to tread*. But I must leave the contrast at the suggestion. One would hardly call Mr. Forster romantic in his treatment of the theme: it would be even more misleading to call Lawrence so, in spite of the strange, remote, terrible beauty of the end:

"And a wild, terrible happiness would take hold of her, beyond despair, but very like despair. No one would ever find her. She had gone beyond the world into the pre-world, she had re-opened the old eternity."

We are left not knowing what is in front of her, but sure that it will not be what we know as happiness.

For whatever the sense in which Lawrence may be called a "romantic," he does not deal in romantic love. The nature of his preoccupation with sex seems to be widely misunderstood. Opposed to the hostile view of him as suffering from sex-obsession is the view some admirers form of him as standing along with the most enlightened sex-reformers for rational, civilised, hygienic enfranchisement from inhibitions. How marvellously these admirers fail to notice what he intends for them! Neither view comes near the truth. There can hardly have been a sterner moralist about sex than Lawrence; it was for him the centre of a religion:

> "But sex was a powerful, potent thing, not to be played with or paraded. The one mystery. And a mystery greater than the individual. The individual hardly counted."[1]

There is nothing seductive here. Indeed, one does not need to be a libertine to find something repellent about it: Lawrence himself supplies the word "inhuman":

> "This is the soul now retreating, back from the outer life of day, back to the origins. And so, it stays its hour at the first great sensual stations, the solar plexus, and the lumbar ganglion. But the tide

[1] *The Plumed Serpent*, p. 162.

ebbs on, down to the immense, almost inhuman passionate darkness of sex, the strange and moon-like intensity of the hypogastric plexus and the sacral ganglion, then deep, deeper, past the last great station of the darkest psyche, down to the earth's centre. Then we sleep.

"And so we resolve back towards our elementals. We dissolve back, out of the upper consciousness, out of mind and sight and speech, back, down into the deep and massive, swaying consciousness of the dark living blood."[1]

This process is necessary before we can find "the great living darkness which we represent by the glyph, God."[2] For

"the human heart must have an absolute. It is one of the conditions of being human. The only thing is the God who is the source of all passion. Once go down before the God-passion and human passions take their right rhythm."[3]

It is necessary

"to refer the sensual passion to the great dark God, the ithyphallic of the first dark religions."[4]

And so "fulfilment" is made possible ("The goal of life is the coming to perfection of each single individual").

"'You learn to be quite alone, and possess your own soul in isolation—and at the same time, to be perfectly *with* someone else—that's all I ask.'

'Sort of sit on a mountain top, back to back with somebody else, like a couple of idols.'

'No—because it isn't a case of sitting. It's what

[1] *Fantasia of the Unconscious*, p. 166.

[2] *Kangaroo*, p. 298.

[3] *Ibid.*, p. 222.

[4] *Ibid.*, p. 226.

you get to after a lot of fighting and a lot of sensual fulfilment. And it never does away with the fighting and with the sensual passion. It flowers on top of them, and it would never flower save on top of them.'"[1]

This is the burden of Lawrence's work from *Aaron's Rod* (1922) onwards. That his religion was a reality to him there can be no doubt. But the reader is oppressed by the terrible monotony associated with it:

"This is the innermost symbol of man: alone in the darkness of the cavern of himself, listening to the soundlessness of inflowing fate."[2]

If the service of the dark God was the condition of Lawrence's magnificently sensuous vitality, and of his power to evoke strange modes of consciousness,[3] then it to that extent justified itself. But it will not produce genius in the rest of us, and his writings are far from constituting presumptive validation of a cult: their imperfections are too significant. Lawrence may affirm that "Emotions by themselves become just a nuisance,"[4] and that

[1] *Aaron's Rod*, p. 111. [2] *Kangaroo*, p. 311.

[3] "Sometimes, in America, the shadow of that old pre-Flood world was so strong, that the day of historic humanity would melt out of Kate's consciousness, and she would begin to approximate to the old mode of consciousness, the old dark will, the unconcern for death, the subtle, dark consciousness, non-cerebral, but vertebrate, when the mind and the power of man was in his blood and his back-bone, and there was the strange, dark intercommunication between man and man and man and beast, from the powerful spine."—*The Plumed Serpent*, p. 443-4.

"In the dark, mindful silence and inflection of the cypress trees, lost races, lost language, lost human ways of feeling and of knowing."—*Aaron's Rod*, p. 277.

[4] *Assorted Articles*, p. 206.

"let man be as primitive as primitive can be, he still has a mind,"[1] but it is plain that the civilisation that he still seems in some way to care for could not exist if no one cared more about "mind" than he does. It is plain that his devotion to the dark God is not so much an evangel of salvation as a symptom; a refuge from the general malady rather than a cure:

> "Away from the burden of intensive mental consciousness. Back into the semi-dark, the half-conscious, the clair-obscur, where consciousness pulsed as a passionate vibration, not as mind-knowledge."[2]

Next in order of publication to *The Lost Girl* comes *Aaron's Rod*. Like the Lost Girl, Aaron Sisson broke with the old life and went to Italy—wandered off in search of "fulfilment."

> "Now he realised that love, even in its intensest, was only an attribute of the human soul."

And he sought to establish relations of "polarity" with a man, one Lilly. This, rather than his relations with women, is the theme of the book. Lilly is undisguised Lawrence, and since Aaron himself is almost as little detached from the writer, the book is naturally a very imperfect work of art. It has all the faults suggested by this:

> "Don't grumble at me then, gentle reader, and swear at me that this damned fellow wasn't half-clever enough to think all these smart things, and realise all these fine-drawn-out subtleties. You are

[1] *Assorted Articles*, p. 205. [2] *Kangaroo*, p. 267.

quite right, he wasn't, yet it all resolved itself in him as I say, and it is for you to prove that it didn't."

Lawrence found it easier to be a novelist in *The Lost Girl*, where he had a heroine instead of a hero. In *Kangaroo* (1923) it is a great deal worse: the novelist suffers ignominious disaster:

"Poor Richard Lovat wearied himself to death struggling with the problem of himself and calling it Australia."

Richard Lovat Somers ("one of the most intensely English little men England ever produced") is frank about it:

"But from this vantage ground let me preach to myself. He preached, and the record was taken down for this gramophone of a novel."

The best part of the book (and this part is very good indeed) makes little pretence of belonging to it: it is a chapter called *The Nightmare*, describing Lawrence's experiences in England during the war. His main concern in the book is to make up his mind whether he can seriously propose to enter the field of action as a prophet with a sworn following. He decides that he cannot.

So, not unnaturally, his next novel, *The Plumed Serpent* (1926), (*The Boy in the Bush*, a work of collaboration, appears to be mainly not his), is largely a day-dream, a wish-fulfilment. It describes a successful attempt to restore the ancient religion of Mexico:

"It was as if, from Ramon and Cipriano, from Jamiltepec and the lake region, a new world was

> unfolding, unrolling, as softly and subtly as twilight falling and removing the clutter of day."

The descriptions of the country and the evocations of "the dark power in the soil" are marvellous, but Lawrence's efforts to persuade himself that he takes the Mexican religion seriously invite the application to himself of certain comments that, in *Studies in Classic American Literature*, he makes on Melville:

> "At first you are put off by the style. . . . It seems spurious and you feel Melville is trying to put something over you. It won't do.
>
> "And Melville really is a bit sententious; aware of himself, self-conscious, putting something over even himself. . . . He preaches and holds forth because he's not sure of himself. And he holds forth, often, so amateurishly."

One cannot but grieve over the dissipation of genius represented by these novels in their careless, hurried redundancy. During the last decade of Lawrence's life his books followed so fast one upon another that it was difficult to keep pace with them. He had a living to make. And this is not the only way in which his faults were the fault of the age. Like Blake, he was doomed to waste his power.

His last novel, however, is not open to the kind of criticism advanced above. *Lady Chatterley's Lover* (1928) is "pure, passionate experience." Compared with the preceding novels, it exhibits a narrowing down; but narrowing down here means also concentration. Lawrence knows exactly what he wants to do and does it perfectly. There is no redundancy in *Lady Chatterley's Lover*, no loose prophecy or passional exegesis, and no mechanical use of the specialised vocabulary. He returns here to the scenes of his early work, and the book has the old sensuous concreteness without the fevered adolescent overcharge: ripe experience is in control. So far as artistic success can validate his teaching *Lady Chatterley's Lover* does so. It magnificently enforces the argument of *Pornography and Obscenity*, and so cannot expect free circulation. But so beautifully poised and sure is the art that there is a danger of mistaking the nature of the success. The success, I have implied, is conditioned by narrowing down: criticism must take the form of the question: How comprehensive or generally valid is this solution?

Can we believe that even the particular, personal problems facing Connie and the gamekeeper are permanently solved (for the gamekeeper is after all not D. H. Lawrence)? As for the general problems, the splendid artistic maturity of *Lady Chatterley's Lover* serves to define our critical reaction to Lawrence's "conclusions" more sharply. And this in spite of the greater maturity that appears also in the latest discursive handling of these conclusions—as in *A propos of Lady Chatterley's Lover*, or here:

"Nowadays we like to talk about spontaneity, spontaneous feeling, spontaneous passion, spontaneous emotion. But our very spontaneity is just an idea. All our modern spontaneity is fathered in the mind, gestated in self-consciousness.

"Since man became a domesticated, thinking animal, long, long ago, a little lower than the angels, he long, long ago left off being a wild instinctive animal. If he ever was such, which I don't believe. In my opinion the most prognathous cave-man was an ideal beast. He ground on his crude, obstinate idea. He was no more like the wild deer or the jaguar among the mountains than we are. He ground his ideas in the slow ponderous mill of his heavy cranium.

"Man is never spontaneous, as we imagine the thrushes or the sparrow hawk, for example, to be spontaneous."[1]

"Emotions by themselves become just a nuisance."[2]

But

"When the Unknown God whom we ignore turns savagely to rend us, from the darkness of oblivion, and when the Life that we exclude from our living turns to poison and madness in our veins, then there is only one thing left to do. We have to struggle down to the heart of things, where the everlasting flame is, and kindle ourselves another beam of light. In short, we have to make another bitter adventure in pulsating thought, far, far to the one central pole of energy. We have to germinate inside us, between our undaunted mind and our reckless, genuine passions, a new germ. The germ of a new idea. A new germ of God-knowledge, or Life-knowledge, but a new germ."[3]

The wisdom here is surer than in the earlier prophetic writings. But, again, it is to the concrete that we go with our questions. And of *Lady Chatterley's Lover* we ask: If we accepted this, and all it implies, without reserves, what should we be

[1] *Assorted Articles*, p. 204. [2] *Ibid.*, p. 206.
[3] *Ibid.*, p. 214.

surrendering? I had in discussion made my point with the random instance that we should be surrendering all that Jane Austen stands for; so when I came across this in *A propos of Lady Chatterley's Lover*, I gave it perhaps undue weight:

> "In the old England, the curious blood-connection held the classes together. The squires might be arrogant, violent, bullying and unjust, yet in some ways there were *at one* with the people, part of the same blood-stream. We feel it in Defoe or Fielding. And then, in the mean Jane Austen, it is gone. Already this old maid typifies 'personality'[1] instead of character, the sharp knowing in apartness, instead of knowing in togetherness, and she is, to my feeling, thoroughly unpleasant, English in the bad, mean, snobbish sense of the word, just as Fielding is English in the good, generous sense."

In any case, Jane Austen is not an adequate symbol, nor one that has, it may be, the same value for Lawrence as for me. But consider instead Mr. E. M. Forster. It seems to me too easily assumed that *Lady Chatterley's Lover* represents greater health and vitality than *A Passage to India*. And if we accepted the first without reserves, how much of what is represented by the second should we have to abandon? It is plain that *A Passage to India* stands for qualities of intelligence and civilisation that Lawrence has little concern for, though (in the person of Richard Lovat Somers) he may reiterate:

> "I won't give up the flag of our real civilised consciousness. I'll give up the ideals. But not the

[1] "The so-called cultured classes are the first to develop 'personality.'"—*A propos of Lady Chatterley's Lover*, p. 58.

aware, self-responsible, deep consciousness that we've gained."[1]

I do not myself believe that we can preserve this "civilised consciousness" without the qualities that are embodied in *A Passage to India.*

Lawrence, in fact, concede what he might to intelligence, ripe wisdom, "mind," "ideas" and "ideals," was never any the less a romantic rebel:

"Those old Africans! And Atlantis! Strange, strange wisdom of the Kabyles! Old, old dark Africa, and the world before the flood."[2]

"I honestly think that the great pagan world of which Egypt and Greece were the last living terms, the great pagan world which preceded our own era once, had a vast and perhaps perfect science of its own, a science in terms of life. In our era this science crumbled into magic and charlatanry. But even wisdom crumbles.

"I believe that this great science previous to ours and quite different in constitution and nature was once universal, established all over the then-existing globe. I believe it was esoteric, invested in a large priesthood. Just as mathematics and mechanics and physics are defined and expounded in the same way in the universities of China or Bolivia or London or Moscow to-day, so, it seems to me, in the great world previous to ours a great science and cosmology were taught esoterically in all countries of the globe, Asia, Polynesia, America, Atlantis and Europe."[3]

And it is amusing to watch him going about the world discovering strange, strange wisdom in remote or primitive people, and suffering furious revulsion

[1] *Kangaroo*, p. 390. [2] *Aaron's Rod*, p. 117.

[3] *Fantasia of the Unconscious*, p. 8.

when his civilised susceptibilities are outraged. But he never fell into disillusion: his splendid genius burned always with a fierce flame. He went always in the conviction that at any moment the veil might be rent, and a new world dawn:

> "The idea, the actual idea must rise ever fresh, ever displaced, like the leaves of a tree, from out of the quickness of the sap, and according to the ever incalculable effluence of the great dynamic centres of life. The tree of life is a gay kind of tree that is for ever dropping its leaves and budding out afresh, quite different ones. If the last lot were thistle leaves, the next lot may be vine. You never can tell with the Tree of Life."[1]

Now this is not the whole of wisdom. There is another part that Lawrence himself recognises distantly:

> "Though here, as everywhere, we must remember that a man has a double set of desires, the shallow and the profound, the personal, superficial, temporary desires, and the inner, impersonal, great desires that are fulfilled in long periods of time."[2]

A complete wisdom, it perhaps hardly needs arguing, involves greater concern for intelligence and the finer products of civilisation than Lawrence ever manifests. Against his preoccupation with primitive consciousness and "the old blood-warmth of oneness and togetherness" his concessions to "ideas" and "mind" show as little more than lip-service.

Lady Chatterley's Lover, in fact, states a problem

[1] *Ibid.*, p. 74. [2] *A propos of Lady Chatterley's Lover*, p. 34.

rather than offers any solution—states magnificently in the concrete the major, the inclusive problem of our time. Contrast with the passage quoted earlier from *The Rainbow* this:

"The car ploughed uphill through the long squalid straggle of Tevershall, the blackened brick dwellings, the black slate roofs glistening their sharp edges, the mud black with coal-dust, the pavements wet and black. It was as if dismalness had soaked through and through everything. The utter negation of natural beauty, the utter negation of the gladness of life, the utter absence of the instinct for shapely beauty which every bird and beast has, the utter death of the human intuitive faculty was appalling. The stacks of soap in the grocer's shops, the rhubarb and lemons in the green-grocers! the awful hats in the milliners! all went by ugly, ugly, ugly, followed by the plaster and gilt horror of the cinema with its wet picture announcements, 'A Woman's Love,' and the new big Primitive chapel, primitive enough in its stark brick and big panes of greenish and raspberry glass in the windows. The Wesleyan chapel, higher up, was of blackened brick and stood behind iron railings and blackened shrubs. The Congregational chapel which thought itself superior, was built of rusticated sandstone and had a steeple, but not a very high one. Just beyond were the new school buildings, expensive pink brick, and gravelled play-ground inside iron railings, all very imposing, and mixing the suggestion of a chapel and a prison. Standard Five girls were having a singing lesson, just finishing the la-me-doh-la exercises and beginning a 'sweet children's song.' Anything more unlike song, spontaneous song, would be impossible to imagine: a strange bawling yell followed the outlines of a tune. It was not like savages: savages have subtle rhythms. It was not like animals: animals *mean* something when they yell. It was like nothing on earth, and it was called singing. Connie sat and listened with her heart in her boots, as Field was filling petrol. What could possibly become of such a people, a people in whom the living intuitive faculty was dead as nails, and only queer mechanical yells and uncanny will-power remained."

* * * * * *

"England my England! But which is *my* England? The stately homes of England make good photographs and create the illusion of a connection with the Elizabethans. The handsome old halls are there, from the days of good Queen Anne and Tom Jones. But smuts fall and blacken on the drab stucco, that has long ceased to be golden. And one by one, like the stately homes, they are abandoned. Now they are being pulled down. As for the cottages of England—there they are—great plasterings of brick dwellings on the hopeless countryside.

"Now they are pulling down the stately homes, the Georgian halls are going. Fritchley, a perfect old Georgian mansion, was even now, as Connie passed in the car, being demolished. It was in perfect repair: till the war the Weatherleys had lived in style there. But now it was too big, too expensive, and the country had become too uncongenial. The gentry were departing to pleasanter places, where they could spend their money without having to see how it was made.

"This is history. One England blots out another. The mines had made the halls wealthy. Now they were blotting them out, as they had already blotted out the cottages. The industrial England blots out the agricultural England. One meaning blots out another. The new England blots out the old England. And the continuity is not organic, but mechanical."

The old rhythms of life have disappeared, the old adjustments of man to the environment and to the conditions of living. The rate of change has far exceeded the powers of readjustment:

> "There was a gap in the continuity of consciousness almost American, but industrial really. What next?"

"Industrialism" is only a subheading of the problem, the fundamental nature of which is suggested by these passages from Spengler:

> "Man as civilised, as *intellectual nomad*, is again wholly microcosmic, wholly homeless, as free *intellectually* as hunter and herdsman were free sensually. '*Ubi bene, ibi patria*' is valid *before* as well as after a *Culture*. In the not-yet-spring of the migrations it was a German yearning—virginal, yet already maternal—that searched the South for a home in which to nest its future culture. To-day, at the end of this culture, the rootless intellect ranges over all landscapes and all possibilities of thought. But between these limits lies the time in which a man held a bit of soil to be something *worth dying for*."[1]
>
> "There, separated from the power of the land—cut off from it, even by the pavement underfoot—Being becomes more and more languid, sensation and reason more and more powerful. Man becomes *intellect*, 'free' like the nomads, whom he comes to resemble, but narrower and colder than they. '*Intellect*,' 'Geist,' 'esprit,' is the specific urban form of the understanding waking-consciousness. All art, all religion and science, become slowly intellectualised, alien to the land, incomprehensible to the peasant of the soil. With the civilisation sets in the climacteric. The immemorially old roots of Being are dried

[1] *The Decline of the West*, Vol. II, p. 90.

up in the stone masses of its cities. And the free intellect—fateful word!—appears like a flame, mounts splendid into the air, and pitiably dies."[1]

One can, without endorsing the Spenglerian idiom or philosophy, recognise the felicity of this as an account of the present situation. The traditional ways of life have been destroyed by the machine, more and more does human life depart from the natural rhythms,[2] the cultures have mingled, and the forms have dissolved into chaos, so that everywhere the serious literature of the West betrays a sense of paralysing consciousness, of a lack of direction, of momentum, of dynamic axioms.

"We have no future; neither for our hopes nor our aims nor our art. It has all gone grey and opaque."[3]

"Vitally, the human race is dying. It is like a great uprooted tree, with its roots in the air. We must plant ourselves again in the universe."[4]

This is everywhere the cry of the sensitive and

[1] *The Decline of the West,* Vol. II, p. 92.

[2] "Oh, what a catastrophe for man when he cut himself off from the rhythm of the year, from his unison with the sun and the earth. Oh, what a catastrophe, what a maiming of love when it was made a personal, merely personal feeling, taken away from the rising and setting of the sun, and cut off from the magic connection of the solstice and the equinox! This is what is the matter with us. We are bleeding at the roots, because we are cut off from the earth and sun and stars, and love is a grinning mockery, because, poor blossom, we plucked it off from its stem on the tree of life, and expected it to keep on blooming in our civilised vase on the table."—*A propos of Lady Chatterley's Lover,* p. 40.

[3] *Fantasia of the Unconscious,* p. 11.

[4] *A propos of Lady Chatterley's Lover,* p. 52.

aware: Spengler merely voices the general sense. His very idiom is often curiously Laurentian:

> "What makes the man of the world-cities incapable of living on any but this artificial footing is that the cosmic beat in his being is ever decreasing, while the tensions of his waking-consciousness become more and more dangerous. It must be remembered that in a microcosm the animal, waking side supervenes upon the vegetable side, that of being, and not vice versa. Beat and tension, blood and intellect, Destiny and Causality are to one another as the countryside in bloom is to the city of stone, as something existing *per se* to something existing dependently. Tension without cosmic pulsation to animate it is the transition to nothingness. But Civilisation is nothing but tension. The head, in all the outstanding men of the Civilisation, is dominated exclusively by an expression of extreme tension. Intelligence is only the capacity for understanding at high tension, and in every Culture these heads are the types of its final men—one has only to compare them with the peasant heads, when such happen to emerge in the swirl of the great city's street life. The advance, too, from peasant wisdom —'slimness,' mother-wit, instinct, based as in other animals upon the sensed beat of life . . . etc."[1]

But the likeness between Lawrence and Spengler goes no further: the comparison ends in contrast. For Lawrence is in himself the strongest argument against Spengler's "philosophy." He represents the splendid human vitality, the creative faith, and the passionate sense of responsibility that make Spengler's fatalism look like an arduously mean

[1] *The Decline of the West*, p. 102.

exercise of self-importance.[1] Looking upon the scene surveyed by Spengler, Lawrence affirms:

> "But this time, it seems to me, we have consciously and responsibly to carry ourselves through the winter period, the period of death and denudation: that is, some of us have, some *nation* even must. For there are not now, as in the Roman times, any great reservoirs of energetic barbaric life. Goths, Gauls, Germans, Slavs, Tartars. The world is very full of people, but all fixed in civilisations of their own, and they all have our vices, all our mechanisms, and all our means of destruction. This time, the leading civilisation cannot die out as Greece, Rome, Persia died. It must suffer a great collapse, may be. But it must carry through all the collapse the living clue to the next civilisation. It is no good thinking we can leave it to China or Japan or India or Africa—any of the great swarms."[2]

The affirmation has weight, for it is implicit in the creative work of a great artist.

As for Lawrence's extravagances about "ideas," "mind-knowledge," science and education, we shall be fairer to him if we juxtapose them with this:

> "Is it too unattainable a social ideal to believe that every man, woman and child should be trained about his own organism as thoroughly as the last boy was trained about the clock? We could very quickly teach children enough anatomy to give them a

[1] "They know our civilisation has got to smash, sooner or later, so they say: 'Let it! But let me live my life first!'

"Which is all very well, but it's a coward's attitude. They say glibly: 'Oh, well, every civilisation must fall at last—look at Rome!' Very good, look at Rome. And what do you see? A mass of 'civilised' so-called Romans, airing their laissez-faire and laisser-aller sentiments."—*Assorted Articles*, p. 210.

[2] *Fantasia of the Unconscious*, p. 163.

thorough working notion of their body, nervous system, heart, lungs, liver, kidneys, glands, sex apparatus. . . .

"Next we should teach the rudiments of hygiene (what may be called 'mental hygiene'), show them in the simplest kind of terms how infantile unverbalised behaviour arises, and how it is carried over into adult life; teach them about fear, love, and anger reactions, work out with them how the individual behaves in depressions. Teach them what exhibition behaviour is like, how easy seclusion behaviour develops, about invalidism and other nascent psychoses. Teach them first to spot these reaction patterns in others, and then, most important of all, how to spot them in themselves by watching and tabulating their own behaviour. What boy or girl taught in this way could not check his own behaviour three or four times a month? 'For days I have fought with my parents—two or three times in the last week I have been depressed and have tried to find excuses for not going to school and doing my work.' . . . Or once more, 'I find that I am going with girls much less than I used to and that I have begun to gang up with boys in the neighbourhood.'

"Having taught individuals to observe their own behaviour in this way, as they observe the behaviour of others, can't we next teach them what to do when their records show that they are getting into jams? In other words, give them the essentials of corrective hygiene. For example: 'All my work has slowed down. I am lacking in pep, don't care whether I go to see anybody or not; I have been leading a humdrum existence, things haven't gone right at home. I guess I'll talk to my physician. He will probably tell me I had better pack up and go for a week's fishing or hunting, and that when I come back I'd better change things around a bit and try to do some interesting jobs, get some hobbies going that I have been flirting with for a long time, and to reach some satisfactory decision about my sex life which has been bothering me lately.'

"I would give this training before the fourteenth year, since at this age the great mass of our population gives up its schooling. Can young children get all this? I am hopeful of it. My business experience has opened my eyes to how simply things can be put to the public—how in homely words nearly all the worth-while truths of science can be set forth."[1]

Juxtaposed with this scientific horse-sense of Dr. John B. Watson, Lawrence's wildest extravagances appear less extravagant. Dr. Watson, of course, is an extreme instance, but he has great influence in America, and it is not for proposals like the above that he is regarded in England as a crank. They merely represent in a pronounced form certain tendencies that are general in the West. And the pronounced form brings home to us that Lawrence had excuses for his prophetic passion. Civilised life is certainly threatened with impoverishment by education based on crude and defective psychology,[2] by standardisation at a low level, and by the inculcation of a cheap and shallow emotional code. Lawrence's genius has done much to make this more widely and more keenly realised than before. It is a great service.

It is to the creative artist mainly that we owe the

[1] J. B. Watson, *The Ways of Behaviourism*, p. 114.

[2] "The fact is, our process of universal education is to-day so uncouth, so psychologically barbaric, that it is the most terrible menace to the existence of our race."—*Fantasia of the Unconscious*, p. 73.

service. To read Lawrence's best work is to undergo a renewal of sensuous and emotional life, and to learn a new awareness. His art is at its surest in books that we have not yet considered: the books of short stories. Here, in *The Ladybird, England my England, St. Mawr* and *The Woman who rode away*, where he has no room for discursive prophecy and is not tempted to dwell upon his "conclusions," his genius triumphs again and again. In the long short-story called *St. Mawr*, for instance, all his teaching is implicit, but inseparable from the art; his main habitual themes are present (the range is wider than that of *Lady Chatterley's Lover*) in intense concentration. The characterisation is done with an amazing sureness, a sureness rarely equalled in the long works. And the horse, St. Mawr, is used with almost incredible success to effect by symbolism what Lawrence has, with great expense of words, again and again failed to do convincingly in the novels.

In such a story as *The Ladybird* we have displayed with perfect art that Laurentian drama of human relationships, the drama of dark antipathies and attractions, of psychic polarities and fields of force, in which we recognise the uncanny insight of genius. Most marvellous of all, perhaps, are things like the title story of *The Woman who rode away*. It has the air of starting in the common world, but it achieves a transmutation of ordinary reality so complete and intense that we have to go to such poetry as *The Ancient Mariner* for parallels. The strangeness is evoked with an immediacy that seems to change the rhythm of the heart. Here Lawrence's romantic genius indulged its bent to the full. But even when he comes nearest to the romanticism of *The Ancient Mariner* it is not, characteristically, in a spirit of day-dream:

> "I like the wide world of centuries and vast ages—mammoth worlds beyond our day, and mankind so wonderful in his distances, his history that has no beginning yet always the pomp and the magnificence of human splendour unfolding through the earth's changing periods. Floods and fire and convulsions and ice-arrest, intervene between the great glamorous civilisations of mankind. But nothing will ever quench humanity and the human potentiality to evolve something magnificent out of a renewed chaos."[1]

The spirit of this may be "romantic," but who will dare to say that this spirit in Lawrence was a weakness? It expresses the courage of strength, and if we cannot share it, we shall at any rate not be tempted to offer as a reason our purer concern for the world as it is.

1930.

* * * * *

Etruscan Places, though not an exciting book, bears interestingly on the question, How much of romantic illusion was there in Lawrence's pre-occupation with primitive peoples of the present and the past? How far did he really deceive himself in the quest that kept him wandering about the

[1] *Fantasia of the Unconscious*, p. 9.

world, from Italy to Australia, from Australia to Mexico, and on? Some measure of self-deception there undoubtedly was in the hope that expressed itself in each fresh setting-out. But it was never for long, if ever, a radical self-deception—the crude hope of picking up (for he certainly believed a casting-back to be necessary) the lost continuity here, or there, in this or that primitive people. The *Letters* make it unmistakably plain (what should in any case have been gathered from the work) that he knew well enough what he was doing.

His migrations were a technique for inner exploration. And so when he says of the Etruscans, "It is as if the current of some strong different life swept through them, different from our shallow current to-day: as if they drew their vitality from different depths that we are denied," we do not inquire very anxiously whether he was right about them or not. What matters is that, in his exposition and commentary, he proves once again so plainly that he himself has access to "different depths that we are denied."

1933.

* * * * *

Some who are most impatient of the traffic in personalities that substitutes for interest in literature turn with eagerness to reminiscences of D. H. Lawrence. I have said elsewhere that he matters because he was a great artist. But the case is not so simple as that might suggest. His art bears a peculiarly close relation to the man—"the man who suffered"—and that is its importance. If we find him great, the supreme importance of his books is perhaps that they assure us that he existed. Those of them which are most successful as art are in some ways saddening and depressing. The fact of personal existence of which they assure us is perhaps the most cheering and enlivening fact the modern world provides. Here was a man with the clairvoyance and honesty of genius whose whole living was an assertion of what the modern world has lost. It is plain from his books that he was not able to maintain steady confident possession of what he sought—wholeness in spontaneity; a human naturalness, inevitable, and more than humanly sanctioned; a sense, religious in potency, of life in continuity of communication with the deepest springs, giving fulfilment in living, "meaning" and a responsive relation with the cosmos. But it is equally plain that he didn't merely seek.

And it appears, too, that his best creative work was not fully representative of him. He himself—the personality behind the best stories—was a less equivocal incitement than these to the recovery of what has been lost. The man appears saner than the art. And how essentially sane are some of those works in the mixed mode—those lyric-expository prophetic extravaganzas, which, for all their preoccupation with the dark gods, are lit with sun. It was not, in any derogatory sense, an abnormal mind that wrote *Apocalypse*.

It may be that Lawrence is approached largely

in a wrong spirit, but it is difficult to believe that his influence can be anything but wholesome, and it is exhilarating to think that in a world of suburbanism, book societies and Marie Stopes he imposed himself. Only those who suppose his message to be that of *The Conquest of Happiness* are likely to see in him the all-sufficing wisdom that will save us. But it is a suspect wisdom that dismisses him in fear or revulsion or contempt. That is why some who a good while ago formed the habit of taking the *Criterion* seriously, now, when they compare the obituary attention given to Harold Monro with that which was given to Lawrence, feel a kind of final depression.

1932.

D. H. LAWRENCE & PROFESSOR IRVING BABBITT[1]

THERE are some writers, a serious interest in whose work leads inevitably to a discussion of their personalities. Mr. Middleton Murry's offence lay not in supposing D. H. Lawrence's personality to be of the importance that justifies public discussion, but in discussing it as he did. In choosing to discuss Lawrence publicly he could have had no stronger endorsement than Mr. Eliot's, and to the importance of D. H. Lawrence there could, perhaps, be no stronger testimony than that Mr. Eliot applauded Mr. Murry's offence. And if, again, one is obliged to be more personal about Mr. Eliot than one would like, that is a testimony to *his* importance.

No one has (and had) dealt with Mr. Murry more appropriately than Mr. Eliot, and yet, of so highly characteristic a performance as *Son of Woman*, he could say (*The Criterion*, July, 1931): "The victim and the sacrificial knife are perfectly adapted to each other." However drastic the criticism that Lawrence, on the accessible evidence, might have seemed to deserve, he did not deserve that. And Mr. Eliot, though he could attest that "Mr. Murry quotes with astonishing accuracy and justice," had, by his own account, an imperfect acquaintance with

[1] *The Letters of D. H. Lawrence*. Edited and with an introduction by Aldous Huxley.

the accessible evidence. The quotation of Mr. Murry's that he repeated, in order to endorse Mr. Murry's characteristic commentary, came from *Lady Chatterley's Lover*, "one of the novels," remarked Mr. Eliot, "which I have not read"—the plea that *Lady Chatterley's Lover* was not accessible would, in more than one way, it is plain, not cover the case. Yet with a lack of caution very remarkable in Mr. Eliot he committed himself to a passionate moral condemnation of Lawrence. Of the passage that he knew only in Mr. Murry's context (a passage from a novel) he remarked: "Such complacent egotism can come only from a very sick soul. . . ." He had already said of Lawrence's history that it was "an appalling narrative of spiritual pride, nourished by ignorance . . .," and, to make the force of the condemnation quite unmistakable, gone on: "had he become a don at Cambridge his ignorance might have had frightful consequences for himself and for the world, 'rotten and rotting others.'" Mr. Eliot should be asking himself earnestly how he can make "an amends" more adequate than the reference in *Thoughts After Lambeth* to Lawrence along with Mr. James Joyce[1] as "two extremely serious and improving writers."

[1] How Lawrence would have taken this coupling is suggested by the following (which is not necessarily fair as criticism): "I had a copy of *Transition*, that Paris magazine—the Amer. number. My God, what a clumsy *olla putrida* James Joyce is! Nothing but old fags and cabbage-stumps of quotations from the Bible and the rest, stewed in the juice of deliberate, journalistic dirty-mindedness—what old and hard-worked staleness, masquerading as the all-new!"

The moral passion that overwhelmed the critic admits, perhaps, only of explanation, but for serious misunderstanding of Lawrence there was every excuse. The novels and the other books do in many ways—in their "Old Moore's Almanacking," as Lawrence calls it (he had no humour, says Mr. Eliot), and their intense and narrow preoccupation —suggest the fanatical eccentric. And even the successful art (the judgment that Lawrence "never succeeded in making a work of art" suggests that Mr. Eliot was indeed content to take a great deal as read) is far from representing the man. Nevertheless, it should have been plain that Lawrence had much more in common with Blake than with Rousseau (the comparison that Mr. Eliot offered Mr. Murry). In fact, Mr. Eliot might have found in an essay on Blake included in a book called *The Sacred Wood*, some admirably said things that might have been said of Lawrence. At any rate, on the lowest estimate of his importance, it should have been plain that Lawrence was for *The Criterion* an opportunity and a test. How it actually economised its obituary honours and distributed its generosity has already been noted in *Scrutiny*.

For several years before the *Letters* came out one's sense that Lawrence was greater than his writings had been steadily growing, as the signs accumulated and understanding increased. The *Letters* confirm that sense with a completeness that could not have been anticipated, at any rate, by those who did not know him. The account of his history as "a narrative of spiritual pride, nourished by ignorance," becomes ridiculous. It is true that from the beginning he had a complete certitude of his genius: "Tell Arnold Bennett," he writes in 1915, "that all rules of construction hold good only for novels which are copies of other novels. A book which is not a copy of others books has its own construction, and what he calls faults, he being an old imitator, I call characteristics. I shall repeat till I am grey—when they have as good work to show, they may make their pronouncements *ex cathedra*. Till then, let them learn decent respect." And three years earlier he had written: "I think, do you know, that I have inside me a sort of answer to the *want* of to-day: to the real, deep want of the English people, not to just what they fancy they want." With such convictions we should expect to find some measure of "complacent egotism."

But of "complacent egotism," in eight hundred and fifty pages of private correspondence, written, unquestionably, with no thought but of the reader addressed, there is not the least sign, and this remarkable fact should in itself suggest that the convictions were not altogether unjustified. And so far from appearing "a very sick soul . . . totally incapable of intimacy," Lawrence shows himself normal, central and sane to the point of genius, exquisitely but surely poised, and with a rare capacity for personal relations. It is true that he writes to Mr. Middleton Murry: "And I very much dislike any attempt at intimacy like the one you had with —— —— and others. When you start that, I only feel: For God's sake let me get clear of him." He also says: "I'm sick to death of people who are wrapped up in their own inner selves, inner lives." But such remarks, Mr. Eliot would agree, are not evidence for his account of Lawrence. Lawrence, so far from being the "impossible" fanatic offered us, shows himself, under all kinds of provocation, beautifully understanding, delicate and forbearing, while never for a moment compromising his integrity. The intense preoccupations of his novels, it is plain, express no narrowness in the man, but rather a resolution to concentrate upon what seemed to him the centre of the problem. But the problem was far from being all of his life. "They simply are," he wrote, "so eaten up with caring. They are so busy caring about Fascism or Leagues of Nations or whether France is right or whether Marriage is threatened, that they never know where they are. They certainly never live on the spot where they are." Lawrence always lived on the spot where he was. That was his genius.

Not that he was careless of the "before and after." His sense of value, like his spiritual insight and his intelligence, was quick and sure. The qualities that made him incapable of self-deception made him the finest literary critic of his time. He had exquisite spiritual manners, and was always grateful for help, but he "placed" Georgian poetry in 1913, and nothing could have induced him to pretend that the Poetry Bookshop was an institution of European importance. We find him in 1913 giving Mr. Edward Marsh, who found fault with his craftsmanship, Dr. Richards's case (essentially that) against prosody, and remarking to someone else that "that *Golden Journey to Samarcand* only took place on paper—no matter who went to Asia Minor." And how delicately he refuses to countenance Mr. Murry's estimate of Katherine Mansfield! Arnold Bennett ("I hate his resignation") he calls "a sort of pig in clover." Mr. Wells—but one could extract a small book of literary criticism from the *Letters*.

Lawrence, then, it turns out, offers a serious "classicism" a severer test than could have been divined. "What true education should do . . .," wrote Mr. Eliot, imagining the frightful consequences of Lawrence's being a don at Cambridge, ". . . is to develop a wise and large capacity for orthodoxy, to preserve the individual from the solely centrifugal impulse of heresy, to make him capable of judging for himself and at the same time capable of judging and understanding the judgments of the experience of the race." That, in the abstract, is wisdom. But much may happen between the abstract and the concrete. And the degeneration, in practice, of such wisdom produces something far more common in the academic world—an incomparably less remote danger—than what Mr. Elior fears in Lawrence: there is a dry rot that anyone may find without much search, "rotten and rotting others."

A "spiritual askesis," "a training of the emotions," tends very readily to get confused with something very different, Professor Irving Babbitt's preoccupation with the "inner check," and that is only a comparatively respectable form of something that prevails in most institutions, academic and other. "I only want to know people who have courage to live," wrote Lawrence. And while he could say, "More and more I admire the true classic dignity and responsibility," he was moved to exclaim, "This classiosity is bunkum, but still more cowardice." Mr. Eliot once remarked how much better Bertrand Russell would have been for an education in the classics. Lawrence wrote in 1915: "What ails Russell is, in matter of life and emotion, the inexperience of youth. He is, vitally and emotionally, much too inexperienced in personal contact and conflict, for a man of his age and calibre. It isn't that life has been too much for him, but too little." The difference in diagnosis is characteristic. The bent represented by Mr. Eliot's prescription, going with fear of Lawrence, would hardly tend to discourage "classiosity."

As Lawrence should have been a test, so now, as revealed in the *Letters* in something like his fulness, he offers us a test to apply. He was, as he says again and again, essentially religious. Mr. Eliot will point out the dangers of a religion that expresses itself in this way: "What intimations of immortality have we, save our spontaneous wishes? God works in me (if I use the term God) as my desire." But the notion that Lawrence was in any way Rousseauistic or romantic would not survive a reading of the *Letters*. "Is there nothing beyond, my fellow man? If not, then there is nothing beyond myself, beyond my throat, which may be cut, and my own purse, which may be slit; because *I* am the fellow-man of all the world, my neighbour is but myself in a mirror. So we toil in a circle of pure egoism." Mr. Eliot himself never exposed Humanitarianism more effectively. And it is Lawrence's greatness that he convinces us of his actually believing in something "beyond his fellow-men." He alone cannot give us the religion for which the human spirit withers, but the fact that he lived and was so is a highly valuable fact. And he helps those of us who, respecting intensely Mr. Eliot's mind and personality, have, though conscious of theological incapacity and lack of experience, attempted to follow his religious utterances, to define our attitude towards them.

Lawrence's preoccupation with sex was religious. Mr. Eliot's religious preoccupations involve an attitude towards sex. Writing on Lawrence in *La Nouvelle Revue Française* for May, 1927, Mr. Eliot wrote: "Quand ses personnages font l'amour . . . non seulement ils perdent toutes les aménités, raffinements et grâces que plusieurs siècles ont elaborés afin de rendre l'amour *supportable*[1] mais ils semblent remonter le cours de l'évolution . . . jusqu'a quelque hideux accouplement de protoplasme." Surely the

[1] Not Mr. Eliot's italics.

rejection of Romantic Love, Love as the Absolute, does not necessarily lead one to *this?* We cannot help connecting the passage with such things as these in Mr. Eliot's introduction to *The Intimate Journals of Baudelaire*, and concluding that here too he speaks for himself: ". . . the recognition of the reality of Sin is a New Life; and the possibility of damnation is itself so immense a relief in a world of electoral reform, plebiscites, sex reform and dress reform, that damnation itself is an immediate form of Salvation—of salvation from the ennui of modern life, because it gives some significance to living" . . . "Having an imperfect, vague, romantic conception of Good, he was at least able to see that to conceive of the sexual act as evil is more dignified, less boring, than to think of it as the natural, 'life-giving,' cheery automatism of the modern world. For Baudelaire, sexual operation is at least something not analogous to Kruschen salts." Is this all there is to the dogma of Original Sin? Does belief in the supernatural depend on that sleight with the word "natural"? Lawrence hated "sex reform" and "cheery automatism" at least as much as Mr. Eliot, but he did not turn against life, or find it necessary to run to damnation to escape ennui. "I always labour at the same thing, to make the sex relation valid and precious, not shameful."

All this is no doubt crude. It is not meant to suggest that Lawrence solved any problem for us, but to suggest why he, more than anyone else in our time, makes it possible to cherish some faith in the future of humanity. If the religious sense that he represents so magnificently cannot be generally recovered it is difficult to think with hope of the future forecast by Dr. Richards: "Being by hypothesis, able to become any kind of mind at will, the question, 'What kind of mind shall I choose to be?' would turn into an experimental matter. . . ." (*Practical Criticism*, p. 347). "Thank God," said Lawrence, "I'm not free, any more than a rooted tree is free." While he said also, "Unless from us the future takes place we are death only," it was in the past that he was rooted. Indeed, in our time, when the gap in continuity is almost complete, he may be said to represent, concretely in his living person, the essential human tradition; to represent, in an age that has lost the sense of it, human normality, as only great genius could.

How different a phenomenon he is from the *Surréalisme* described in this number[1] of *Scrutiny* by Monsieur Henri Fluchère does not need elaborating. Of that kind of revolt (however sincere) Lawrence says: "they want to destroy every scrap of tradition and knowledge, which is silly." This, again, is relevant: "And yet affection and trust and even morality are not in themselves a swindle. One can't live without them."

And those who, the plight of the world being what it is, are impatient of any preoccupation with other than economic issues, would do well to ponder this: "Don't think of me as a raving, impractical, vain

[1] December, 1932.

individual. *To be material at this juncture is hopeless, hopeless—or worse than impractical.*"

It remains to add that we are all heavily in Mr. Aldous Huxley's debt, and that the index, so necessary, is almost perfect.

1932.

"UNDER WHICH KING, BEZONIAN?"

PISTOL—*Under which king, Bezonian? speak, or die.*
KING HENRY IV. Part II. Act V. Sc. III.

IT would be very innocent of us to be surprised by the frequency with which we are asked to "show our colours," but the source of the command does sometimes surprise us. Indeed, this very formulation came first from Mr. George Santayana, and others whom we respect have repeated it, in substance, since. We should have thought that we had amply made out our case (if that were needed) for holding the assertion and application of serious standards in literary criticism to be an essential function, and one disastrously inoperative now.

Not that we suppose the service of this function to be the whole duty of man, or our own whole duty. The more seriously one is concerned for literary criticism the less possible does one find it to be concerned for that alone. *Scrutiny* has not, as a matter of fact, confined itself to literary criticism. But to identify *Scrutiny* with a social, economic or political creed or platform would be to compromise and impede its special function. This, in its bearing on the challenge now in view, has already been glossed by: "the free play of intelligence on the underlying issues." More, of course, needs saying. What is immediately in place is to insist that one does not necessarily take one's social and political responsibilities the less seriously because one is not quick to see salvation in a formula or in any simple creed. And it is unlikely that anyone actively and sympathetically interested in *Scrutiny* (whether as a reader or otherwise) will exhibit this kind of quickness. On the other hand, those of us who are particularly engrossed by the business of carrying on *Scrutiny* should perhaps resolve (though it seems unnecessary) to warn ourselves now and then against making the perception of the complexity of problems an excuse for complacent inattention: special duties are not ultimately served by neglect of the more general. But the special function of *Scrutiny* is an indispensable one, and there appears to be no danger of its being excessively attended to.

Sympathisers, then, may be, and, no doubt, are, of varying social, political and economic persuasions. But the function indicated would hardly have been fully realised if its bearing on such persuasions were left at this, no more immediate and particular than has yet been suggested. If there seems to be no reason why supporters of *Scrutiny* should not favour some kind of communism as the solution of the economic problem, it does not seem likely (there is no thought here of Mr. Middleton Murry) that they will be orthodox Marxists. The efficiency of the Marxist dialectic, indeed, makes it difficult to determine what precisely orthodoxy is (we do not find even Mr. Maurice Dobb, whom Mr. Eliot singles out for commendation, very lucid). But there can be no doubt that the dogma of the priority of economic conditions, however stated, means a complete disregard for—or, rather, a hostility towards—the function represented by *Scrutiny*.

Why the attitude expressed in the varying formula that makes "culture" (a term to be examined) derivative from the "methods of production"—why this attitude must be regarded as calamitous Trotsky himself brings out in his *Literature and Revolution*. This book shows him to be a cultivated as well as an unusually intelligent man (which perhaps has something to do with his misfortune). But he too, unhappily, like all the Marxists, practises, with the familiar air of scientific rigour, the familiar vague, blanketing use of essential terms. He can refer, for instance, to the "2nd of August, 1914, when the maddened power of bourgeois culture let loose upon the world the blood and fire of an imperialistic war" (p. 190). This, however, is perhaps a salute to orthodoxy. And it would not be surprising if he had thought it wise to distract attention, if possible, from such things as the following, which uses "culture" very differently, and is hardly orthodox: "The proletariat is forced to take power before it has appropriated the fundamental elements of bourgeois culture; it is forced to overthrow bourgeois society by revolutionary violence, for the very reason that society does not allow it access to culture" (p. 195). The aim of revolution, it appears, is to secure this accursed bourgeois culture for the proletariat. Or, rather, Trotsky knows that behind the word "culture" there is something that cannot be explained by the "methods of production" and that it would be disastrous to destroy as "bourgeois." To assert this un-Marxian truth is the aim of his book. "The proletariat," he says (p. 186), "acquires power for the purpose of doing away with class culture and to make way for human culture." And he insists that the necessary means to this consummation is to maintain continuity. That is, he knows, and virtually says, that "human culture" at present is something covered by "bourgeois culture," the Marxian blanket.

But even Trotsky, although he can speak of the need to "turn the concept of culture into the small change of individual daily living" and can say that "to understand and perceive truly not in a journalistic way but to feel to the bottom the very section of time in which we live, one has to know the past of mankind, its life, its work, its struggles, its hopes, . . ." cannot (or may not) realise the delicate organic growth that "human culture" is. Otherwise he could not so cheerfully contemplate fifty years (p. 190) of revolutionary warfare, during which everything must be subordinated to proletarian victory, and assume, without argument, that the result will be a society in which "the dynamic development of culture will be incomparable with anything that went on in the past" (p. 189). But perhaps, and "dynamic" strongly suggests it, "culture" again means something different.

Indeed, Trotsky at this point in the argument, like all the Marxists, becomes indistinguishable from Mr. Wells. Neither of them has faced the problem, though Trotsky, unlike Mr. Wells, appears capable of seeing it if it is put. A Marxist intelligent enough and well-enough educated to speak of a "human culture" that must, if it is to exist at all, carry on from what orthodoxy dismisses as "bourgeois culture," can hardly have failed to divine that, if he thought too much, not only his orthodoxy but his optimism would be in danger. Nothing brings out more strongly that orthodox Marxists (like most other publicists) use the word "culture" uncomprehendingly than their failure even to perceive the problem—the problem that their dogma concerning the relation between culture and the "methods of production" confronts them with in a particularly sharp form.

It confronts us all. For it is true that culture in the past has borne a close relation to the "methods of production." A culture expressing itself in a tradition of literature and art—such a tradition as represents the finer consciousness of the race and provides the currency of finer living—can be in a healthy state only if this tradition is in living relation with a real culture, shared by the people at large. The point might be enforced by saying (there is no need to elaborate) that Shakespeare did not invent the language he used. And when England had a popular culture, the structure, the framework, of it was a stylisation, so to speak, of economic necessities; based, it might fairly be said, on the "methods of production" was an art of living, involving codes, developed in ages of continuous experience, of relations between man and man, and man and the environment in its seasonal rhythm. This culture the progress of the nineteenth century destroyed, in country and in town; it destroyed (to repeat a phrase now familiar) the organic community. And what survives of cultural tradition in any important sense survives in spite of the rapidly changing "means of production."

All this seems fairly obvious, and what should be equally obvious is the new status and importance of leisure. Leisure (however much or little there might be) mattered less when work was not, as it is now for so many, the antithesis of living. (See, e.g George Bourne, *Change in the Village*, pp. 200–216.) Now, unless one is unusually lucky, one saves up living for after working hours, and for very few indeed can the bread-winning job give anything like a sense of fulfilment or be realised as in itself a signficant part of a significant process. Marxists do not contemplate any reversal of this development; nor is enthusiasm for Five Year Plans, the sense of a noble cause, or romantic worship of mechanical efficiency, to be permanently the sanction of labour in itself unsatisfying. "The Revolution," writes A. L. Morton, a Marxist, in the October[1]

[1] 1932.

Criterion, "neither creates nor is intended to create a new leisure class. It is intended rather to create a leisure community. . . ." The Marxist, then, who offers his Utopia as anything better than Mr. Wells's, must face the problem that we should all be facing. For any reasonable hope for civilisation must assume that the beneficent potentialities of machine-technique will be realised, and there seems no reason to doubt that the material means of life might be assured to all at the cost of small labour to each.

The problem is suggested by Mr. Morton here: "The state of poetry is largely dependent upon the connection of the leisure class with the productive powers. The connection must be close and vital, though that of the individual poet need not be, since he expresses less himself than his social environment. The great ages of poetry have been those in which the poetry-producing class was young and vigorous and was breaking through existing productive relationships. Conversely, a class without social functions tends to produce decadent poetry." Without being uncritical of Mr. Morton's generalisations one may ask: What will "social functions" be in a leisure community—a community, that is, in which the "productive process" is so efficient as no longer to determine the ordering of life? Mr. Morton speaks of a "leisure community integrally associated with the productive forces in a way in which no one class has ever been before"; but there is surely no particular virtue in being "associated" with productive forces so mechanically efficient that "integrally," here, seems to mean very little? No doubt when we are all leisured the special moral disadvantage of belonging to a leisure class will be gone, but "social function," it is plain, means so much more in the generalisations about culture and the productive process that it is inapplicable here, or, if applied, becomes a mere arbitrary counter. It is a comment on the Marxian dialectic that it can take a man in this way up to the problem and leave him unable to see it.

The problem faces us all, and not hypothetically, but practically and immediately. It is a more difficult one than Trotsky, that dangerously intelligent Marxist who has some inkling, suggests in his statement of it (p. 193): "The main task of the proletarian intelligentsia in the immediate future is not the abstract formation of a new culture regardless of the absence of a base for it, but definite culture-bearing, that is, a systematic, planful, and, of course, critical imparting to the backward masses of the essential elements of the culture which already exists." The problem is, rather, not merely to save these "essential elements" from a swift and final destruction in the process that makes Communism possible,[1] but to develop them into an autonomous

[1] "Industrialisation is desirable not for itself, but because Communism is only possible in an industrial community." A. L. Morton, *The Criterion*, October, 1932. Cf. "The essential point is that agriculture ought to be saved and revived because agriculture is the foundation for the Good Life in any society; it is, in fact, the normal life. . . . And it is hardly too much to say that only in a primarily agricultural society, in which people

culture, a culture independent of any economic, technical or social system as none has been before. Whether such a rootless culture (the metaphor will bear pondering, in view of the contrast between the postulated communist society—in constant "dynamic" development—and any that has produced a culture in the past) can be achieved and maintained may be doubtful. If it cannot, we have nothing better to hope for than a world of Mr. Wells's men like gods, and have rather to fear that the future has been forecast in California.[1] If it can, it will be by a concern for the tradition of human culture, here and now, intenser than Trotsky's (the Marxist excommunicate); a concerted and sustained effort to perpetuate it, in spite of the economic process, the triumphs of engineering and the Conquest of Happiness, as something with its own momentum and life, more and more autonomous and self-subsistent. And in its preoccupation with this effort *Scrutiny* does not find itself largely companied.

This plea, however, will not bring us off; we have no illusions. There is a choice; we must speak or die: Stalin or the King by Divine Right? And the Marxist dialectic, with its appearance of algebraic rigour, stern realism and contemptuous practicality, has great advantages—in dialectic—over those who are pusillanimous enough to let themselves be

have local attachments to their small domains and small communities, and remain, generation after generation, in the same place, is genuine patriotism possible. . . . ." T. S. E., *The Criterion*, October, 1931.

[1] See *Star-Dust in Hollywood*, by J. and C. Gordon.

bothered by the duty and difficulty of using words precisely. The rigour, of course, is illusory, and, consequently, so are the realism and the practicality. "In general," says Mr. Edmund Wilson approvingly in the *New Statesman and Nation* for October 15th, "it is surprising how promptly the writers are lining up in one or other of the camps, and how readily their antagonisms are developing." When people line up so promptly one suspects, not only that the appeal of the *chic* has something to do with it, but that the differences are not of a kind that has much to do with thinking; and the ready development of antagonisms among those whose differences are inessential should surprise only the very innocent.

Trotsky's use of the term "culture" has already been noted. It is part of what Mr. Wilson calls the "Marxist technique"; he himself speaks of the "old bourgeois culture" and the "culture of Marxism." "Bourgeois" and "class," likewise, are primary indispensables of the technique. Prince Mirsky, in his celebrated essay in *Echanges* (December, 1931), dealing with "la poésie bourgeoise," takes as "le poète bourgeois" Mr. T. S. Eliot. He exhibits less acuteness—or (and very naturally) more orthodoxy—than Trotsky, who would hardly have been naïve enough to pronounce (though he does contradict himself, and is capable, he also, of sentimentality): "La bourgeoisie est vide de valeurs, toutes les valeurs vivantes sont du côté de la classe ouvrière." The "values" of the working class (though, of course, one never knows what definitions the Marxist, when challenged, will produce from under the blanket) are inevitably those induced by the modern environment —by "capitalist" civilisation; essentially those, that is, of the "bourgeoisie" and of most Marxists. Mr. Wilson (to illustrate this last point), a critic intelligent enough at his best to have written the best parts of *Axel's Castle*, was capable of resting the structure of that book on the values of the "man who does things," and, seeing that he had thus proclaimed himself a contemporary of Dr. John B. Watson, we ought not to have been surprised when he came out as an admirer of Kipling and innocently assumed that Lytton Strachey was a great writer.

Prince Mirsky, although, presumably, he does not enjoy Mr. Wilson's advantage of having been born to the English language, has over Mr. Wilson the advantage of living in London. He would not, as Mr. Wilson has (see the *New Statesman and Nation*), have solemnly endorsed the collocation of "Dostoevsky, Cervantes, Defoe and E. E. Cummings. . . ." And he may have a good critical sensibility. But that is not proved by his exposition, intelligent and adroit as it is, of Mr. Eliot's poetry. What he certainly shows is unusual skill in applying the "Marxist technique," and the way in which in explaining *The Waste Land* he seizes on the "structural symbols," *l'Humide, le Sec et le Feu*, and overstresses their function, paying little attention to the essential organisation, betrays the influence of the Marxian training. But the significantly betraying thing is the footnote: "les lecteurs d'Edith Sitwell sont en grande partie les mêmes que ceux de Bertrand Russell dont les *Principles of Mathematics* sont l'évangile des logistes." Mathematicians are often illiterate, and Bertrand Russell wrote *The Conquest of Happiness*, and Prince Mirsky might as aptly have said that the readers of Edith Sitwell are in great part the same as those of Ernest Hemingway.

The relevance of this further appeal to performance in literary criticism should not need urging. To be concerned, as *Scrutiny* is, for literary criticism is to be vigilant and scrupulous about the relation between words and the concrete. The inadequacies of Mr. Wilson and Prince Mirsky as literary critics are related to their shamelessly uncritical use of vague abstractions and verbal counters. What is this "bourgeois culture" that Mr. Eliot represents in company, one presumes, with Mr. Wells, Mr. Hugh Walpole, *Punch*, *Scrutiny*, Dr. Marie Stopes and the *Outline for Boys and Girls?* What are these "classes," the conflict between which a novelist must recognise "before he can reach to the heart of any human situation"? (See *Literary Criticism and the Marxian Method* by Granville Hicks in *The Modern Quarterly* for Summer, 1932). The Marxist, of course, is pat with his answer: he will define class in terms of relation to the "productive process." The concept so defined—how usefully and how adequately to the facts this is not the place to discuss—will at any rate, engage with its context. But when one comes to talk of "bourgeois culture" the context has changed, and only by virtue of the Marxist dogma and the Marxist dialectic is it possible to introduce the concept here and suppose one is saying anything. Class of the kind that can justify talk about "class-culture" has long been extinct.[1] (And, it might be added, when there was such "class-culture" it was much more than merely of the class). The process of civilisation that produced, among other things, the Marxian dogma, and makes it plausible, has made the cultural difference between the "classes" inessential. The essential differences are indeed now definable in economic terms, and to aim at solving the problems of civilisation in terms of the "class war" is to aim, whether wittingly or not, at completing the work of capitalism and its products, the cheap car, the wireless and the cinema. It is not for nothing that Trotsky's prose, when he contemplates the "dynamic development of culture" that will follow the triumph of Revolution, takes on a Wellsian exaltation (see e.g. pp. 188–9), and that, when he descends to anything approaching particularity, what he offers might have come from *Men Like Gods* (see p. 252). And the title of Prince Mirsky's essay, *T. S. Eliot et la Fin de la Poésie Bourgeoise*, should have been one word shorter.

The rigour of the Marxian dialectic, then, is illusory, and the brave choice enjoined upon us the

[1] Prince Mirsky refers to "la classe où appartenait Donne"; but what has that "bourgeoisie" in common with that of the Victorian age or that of to-day?

reverse of courageous, if courage has anything to do with thinking. Must we therefore take the other alternative offered us: "si le poète—l'idéologue—bourgeois veut opposer à la Révolution quelque chose de positif et de convaincant (de convaincant pour son propre esprit) il ne peut avoir de recours qu'à la résurrection de quelque revenant médiéval . . . ."? Must we be Royalists and Anglo-Catholics? In the first place, reasons have been advanced for doubting whether those who find Marxism convincing, for their own minds, are applying minds in any serious sense to the problems that face us and them. So if, while agreeing that the recovery of religious sanctions in some form seems necessary to the health of the world, we reply that they cannot be had for the wanting, the Marxist had better not start to think before he twits us with ineffectiveness. And as for Anglo-Catholicism and Royalism, those who may find these, *pour leurs propres esprits*, convincing do not convince us that they are taking up an effective attitude towards the problems. The impressive statement, in the abstract, of a coherent position is not enough. And the main reply to the gesture that bids us, if we respect ourselves, line up there, as the logical and courageous alternative, is not that *The Principles of Modern Heresy* and *The Outline of Royalism* have not yet, after all, been given us, but: "Look at the *Criterion*."

The Editor's spare—too spare—contributions almost always exhibit the uncommon phenomenon of real thinking turned upon the "underlying issues," though, in their bearing on concrete problems, they show no signs of coming any nearer than before to effective particularity. But we must not, under Marxian incitement, suggest unfair tests. The effective particularity we can fairly demand would involve maintaining in the *Criterion* high standards of thinking and of literary criticism. The point that it is necessary to make is, in view of our own enterprise, a delicate one, but only the more necessary for that. Let us suffer the retort when, and as much as, we may deserve it, and express now the general regret that the name of the *Criterion* has become so dismal an irony and that the Editor is so far from applying to his contributors the standards we have learnt from him.

The relevance of the point may be enforced by remarking the particular weakness of the *Criterion* for the dead, academic kind of abstract "thinking," especially when the "thinker" (incapable of literary criticism) stands in a general, abstract way for "order," "intelligence" and the other counters, all of which are worth less than nothing if not related scrupulously to the concrete.

The Marxist challenge, then, seems to us as heroic as Ancient Pistol's and to point to as real alternatives. And we do not suppose that, in *Scrutiny*, we, more than anyone else, have a solution to offer. But, looking round, we do think that, without presuming too much, we can, since there seems no danger of too great an intensity of concern for them, make it our function to insist on certain essential conditions of a solution. Nor, inadequate as our insistence may be, does it appear superfluous to insist that the essential problems should be faced.

Nothing more (if it lived up to this account) should be needed to justify *Scrutiny*. But if some more immediate engaging upon the world of practice would reassure, then we can point to it. We have a special educational interest, and the association of this with the bent already described is unprecedented and has already shown its strength.

RESTATEMENTS FOR CRITICS

CRITICAL attention is something to be grateful for, even when it is as pettish in animadversion as "Ille Ego's" review of *Scrutiny* in *The New English Weekly* for January 5th. This is not to be ungrateful for the generous notice that we have been so widely accorded: warm acknowledgments are due. Nor is it to flatter "Ille Ego" with the suggestion that his comments are very subtle or profound: his pettishness betrays itself, in the familiar ways, as one of the familiar manifestations of uneasily ambitious immaturity. But the misunderstandings he exhibits in naïve forms have, we know, from spoken criticism and from correspondence, a fairly representative quality, and we tender him thanks for the occasion he provides.

Scrutiny, he complains, refuses to be committed. Instead of giving honest and undivided allegiance to its true "god," T. S. Eliot, from whom it "obviously derives" (like most else in "literary Cambridge these past ten years") it goes whoring after D. H. Lawrence, Worse than that, it was conceived in sin, and it has from birth onwards denied its god: "It has its origin in a desire not to be committed to Mr. Eliot," or to any other god or prophet. "It is very definitely not-committed. Indeed, its primary concern appears to be precisely that: to avoid being committed."

To what, it might be asked, is "Ille Ego"

committed? Anyway, "very definitely," to knowing the ante-natal history of *Scrutiny* and the "reality" of Blake, D. H. Lawrence and T. S. Eliot. Under three of these heads, at least, we admit to being much less "committed." But the more naïve self-committals of "Ille Ego" may be left to themselves. When he is usefully representative is when he puts his fundamental incomprehension in so plausible a form as this: "The distinction is suggested in the title. The *Criterion* judges; *Scrutiny* scrutinises. Compared to judgment, scrutiny is a non-committal occupation."

We stand self-condemned, then, by the modesty of our title, by our very lack of pretension. Yet title and pretension are not everything. Forbearing the inquiry whether *Scrutiny* has committed itself less often and less decisively than any other journal in particular judgments, let us ask what, where judgment is in question, the criterion is: what are the standards? The values of intelligence, tradition and orthodox Christianity? But judgment is not a matter of abstractions; it involves particular immediate acts of choice, and these do not advance the business of judgment in any serious sense unless there has been a real and appropriate responsiveness to the thing offered. Without a free and delicate receptivity to fresh experience, whatever the criterion alleged, there is no judging, but merely negation. And this kind of negation, persisted in, with no matter what righteous design, produces in the end nullity: the "criterion," however once validated by experience, fades into impotent abstraction, the "values" it represents become empty husks. The safety sought in this way proves to be the safety of death.

Of course there is more to be said; there is another side. It is not wisdom that stops at advocating the free play of individual sensibility. Indeed, the truly living sensibility cannot be content to be merely individual and merely free. One cannot suppose it either possible or desirable to go on "experiencing" as if there had been nothing before. And with the beginnings of maturity the problem of organisation becomes one for serious effort; taken seriously, it leads to a discipline and a training, emotional and intellectual, designed to "preserve the individual from the solely centrifugal impulse of heresy, to make him capable of judging for himself, and at the same time capable of judging and understanding the judgments of the experience of the race." But this is no matter of simple acceptance or conformity. It is part of our great debt to Mr. Eliot that he has made it so plain that there can be no easy way or simple solution. Of tradition he wrote: "It cannot be inherited, and if you want it you must obtain it by great labour." But it is just our criticism of the *Criterion* that so many of its writers are condemned by the spirit of this dictum. Judgment cannot be a matter of applying the accepted (or "inherited") standards, any more than thinking can be a matter of moving the recognised abstractions according to rule.

Again, in his essay on Massinger, Mr. Eliot wrote: "What may be considered corrupt or decadent in the morals of Massinger is not an alteration or diminution in morals; it is simply the disappearance of all the personal and real emotions which this morality supported and into which it introduced a kind of order. As soon as the emotions disappear the morality which it ordered appears hideous. Puritanism itself became repulsive only when it appeared as the survival of a restraint after the feelings which it restrained had gone." The bearing of this upon (say) a grave and persistent lack, in a journal standing for order, intelligence and orthodoxy, of critical sensitiveness to contemporary literature—to literature and art in general—does not need elaborating, perhaps.

Our criticism, then, is no repudiation of our debt to Mr. Eliot (and the *Criterion*), but the reverse. Nor when we suggest that D. H. Lawrence should have been a test is it necessary, or intelligent, to conclude that we have transferred our allegiance to D. H. Lawrence. "But to *use* Eliot to escape the reality of Lawrence," pronounces "Ille Ego," "and to use Lawrence to escape the reality of Eliot, is to insult both of them."—To suggest that one should "accept" Mr. Eliot or D. H. Lawrence is to insult both of them, it might be retorted, by gross incomprehension, for, whatever the "reality" of either may be, it is certainly such that to contemplate "accepting" it is to repudiate it. The reality of Mr. Eliot in one sense is just what is in question. And to propose Lawrence as a test is not to suggest that Lawrence's reality is simple, a matter for allegiance, loyalty or acceptance. An intelligent, that is, a respectful, attitude towards him must necessarily be a discriminating one; for though "Ille Ego" speaks of Lawrence's "philosophy" as something to be accepted or rejected, those who have read what Lawrence wrote know that he was inconsistent, and inconsistent in such ways that to think of systematising him is to betray a complete obtuseness to his significance.

What Lawrence offers us is not a philosophy or an *œuvre*—a body of literary art—but an experience, or, to fall back on the French again, an *expérience*, for the sense of "experiment" is needed too. In him the human spirit explored, with unsurpassed courage, resource and endurance, the representative, the radical and central problems of our time. Of course he went into dangerous places, and laid himself open to reprehension as setting dangerous examples and inciting to dangerous experiments. But if he earned reprehension, we owe him gratitude for earning it.

More than one summing-up is possible, and it would be absurd to demand agreement with one's own; the stress will fall here for some and there for others. But especially by those who stand for "order" should he have been recognised as a test: a refusal on their part to consider him seriously must appear a very bad sign indeed. And to take the easy recourse of dismissing him in a plausible, too plausible, bracket with Rousseau, or to use Mr. Murry against him, amounts to such a refusal. The reluctant conclusion is at last compelled that the insidious corruptions attendant upon "classicism" have not been sufficiently guarded against; that "order" and "tradition" have ceased to be a living tension, a strenuous centrality, and have become something very different.

"Ille Ego" complains that we desert "at the point where Eliot becomes the orthodox Christian. That, as might have been expected, is too much for Cambridge." But what *is* orthodox Christianity? (And is "Ille Ego" "committed" to it?) If it means the kind of rejection of life implicit in Mr. Eliot's attitude towards sex, then we do certainly dissociate ourselves at that point. Lawrence's preoccupation with sex seems to us much less fairly to be called "obsession" than Mr. Eliot's, and very much preferable. And we know that many who profess Christian sympathies share this view.

If we go on to say that it does not follow that we accept any Laurentian religion we shall, perhaps, not now be taunted with cowardly evasiveness. What, indeed, was Lawrence's religion? "Curse the Strachey," he wrote during the War, "who asks for a new religion—the greedy dog. He wants another juicy bone for his soul, does he? Let him start to fulfil what religion we have." To talk of the "religious sense" that he represents may sound weak, but it should not to those who have read the *Letters*. For many to-day the essential thing is to meet such a sense in the concrete, dominating ("I am a passionately religious man"), and unmistakably an expression of health, courage and vitality. And we meet it, we find, in Lawrence—in the Lawrence who has the right to exclaim as he does against "glib irreverence," because all his writing exhibits reverence as a fact, a fact of honesty, strength and sensitiveness; the Lawrence who disturbs complacency about "sex reform" so much more potently than Mr. Eliot.

This is not to pronounce against the ultimate necessity of theologies, creeds and rituals: it is probable that *Scrutiny* enjoys, and will enjoy, support from readers who profess and practise. But most, we imagine, who respond to Lawrence's "one must speak for life and growth, amid all this mass of destruction and disintegration" find the possibility of adhesion to any formal religion a remote one—as remote as a satisfying answer to the question, What does such adhesion mean in effect? Does, for instance, a declaration of "faith in death" mean a negative acquiescence in the drift of things here below, or, as it might, the opposite?

We have at any rate some notion of the test. And we know that, in such a time of disintegration as the present, formulæ, credos, abstractions are extremely evasive of unambiguous and effective meaning, and that, whatever else may be also necessary, no effort at integration can achieve anything real without a centre of real consensus—

such a centre as is presupposed in the possibility of literary criticism and is tested in particular judgments. But "tested" does not say enough; criticism, when it performs its function, not merely expresses and defines the "contemporary sensibility"; it helps to form it. And the function of *Scrutiny*, as we conceive it, is (among other things) to help to persuade an effective "contemporary sensibility" into being—for that, rather, is what the critical function looks like when decay has gone so far.

The peculiar importance of literary criticism has by now been suggested; where there is a steady and responsible practice of criticism a "centre of real consensus" will, even under present conditions, soon make itself felt. Out of agreement and disagreement with particular judgments of value a sense of relative value in the concrete will define itself, and, without this, no amount of talk about "values" in the abstract is worth anything. And it is not merely a matter of literature ("It would appear that 'literary appreciation' is an abstraction and pure poetry a phantom"—T. S. Eliot, *Selected Essays*, p. 257): there is hardly any need to illustrate the ways in which judgments of literary value involve extra-literary choices and decisions. It should at any rate be enough to suggest that those who differ philosophically and theologically—who differ about religious "beliefs"—may agree that Mr. Eliot and D. H. Lawrence both (however one may "place" them relatively) demand serious attention, and that the supersession by Book Society standards of the standards that compel this judgment will, if not fiercely and publicly resisted, be a disaster for civilisation.

Such consensus can, and must, test and justify itself in action. Above all there are, or we should determine that there shall be, immediate consequences in education: at any rate, the determination, resolutely pursued, would provoke real agreement and real differences. This (need it be said?) is not to show contempt for creed and theory, or to suggest that the function represented by, for example, the *Criterion*, is unnecessary. But what we propose does seem to us certainly necessary if creed is not to be merely debilitating and theory a relapse upon the wrong kind of abstraction, inert and unprofitable.

The Marxist, however, will still protest that (as one correspondent puts it) we are invoking education in order "to escape the urge to political action." It is of no use, it would seem, while he remains a Marxist, to reply that we do not offer education as an alternative. We cannot, it is true, look forward with any hope to bloody revolution, but we are not (again, need it be said?) politically indifferent. It seems appropriate here to speak in the first person. Let me say, then, that I agree with the Marxist to the extent of believing some form of economic communism to be inevitable and desirable, in the sense that it is to this that a power-economy of its very nature points, and only by a deliberate and intelligent working towards it can civilisation be saved from disaster. (The question is, communism of what kind? Is the machine—or Power—to triumph or to be triumphed over, to be the dictator or the servant of human ends?)

When I add that I believe one cannot reasonably pretend to lay down what are the right immediate steps without consulting specialists, and that one of the functions of *Scrutiny* is to provide criteria, from the realm of general intelligence, for determining which specialists can be trusted, and how far, the Marxist will smile. I can only reply, by way of earnest, that a serious educational movement will inevitably, and, as far as I am concerned, explicitly, aim at fostering in schools and in education generally, an anti-acquisitive and anti-competitive moral bent, on the ground (there are others) that the inherited code is disastrously and obviously inappropriate to modern conditions.

But this is not said in any hope of conciliating the Marxist, for he it is who insists on the one thing, the one necessary preoccupation: to confess to a sense of complexities is to play the bourgeois game. Thus our correspondent complains: "you refuse to admit that 'art' and 'culture' are among the chief instruments of oppression—a form of dope. Or if you recognise this . . . you are scornful at the idea that Eliot *and* Walpole, Wells, *Punch*, *Scrutiny*, Stopes and the *Outline for Boys and Girls* are all manifestations of bourgeois culture. I contend that they are—and Eliot seems to me as typical as

Punch, but 'at a different level of appeal' (or 'sensitiveness' or 'intelligence')."—Marxism is indeed, to adapt Lenin's adaptation of the "dope" formula, the alcohol of the intellectual, warming and exalting, obliterating difficulties, and incapacitating for elementary discriminations. After the passage just quoted, one is not surprised to get a defence of Prince Mirsky's "*toutes les valeurs vivantes sont du côté de la classe ouvrière,*" for to include Mr. Eliot and *Punch* under "bourgeois" is to empty the term "value" of all serious meaning.

It is true that one might call not only *Punch* and Mr. Walpole, but also Mr. Eliot and D. H. Lawrence "products" of capitalist civilisation, in that the use made by these two last of their talents was determined by the environment into which they were born. But rejection, after all, is not the same as acceptance, and it is a bourgeois incapacity that cannot recognise the human values that Mr. Eliot and Lawrence, in their different ways, are asserting against the environment—very different ways, and if the values are different too, they are alike in being equally not generated in the modern economic process. Indeed, this is our criticism, that in the matter of "values" the Marxist is too bourgeois, too much the product of the material environment. It is impossible to believe that he who is so obtuse to essential distinctions means anything when he speaks of the "culture" that will supervene upon a politico-economic revolution: the finer human values have, so far as his sense of them goes, been left behind for good in capitalist Progress.

The simplifying dialectic itself works like a machine. "You are quite right," says the correspondent already quoted, "in stating that 'the dogma of the priority of economic conditions means a complete disregard for—or hostility towards—the functions represented by *Scrutiny*.' Orthodox Marxists (i.e. Leninist Marxists) would be hostile to *Scrutiny* . . . .," and he goes on to stigmatise as a "*contre-sens*" our talking of a culture that will have a "momentum and life of its own" when we have admitted that "the economic process must profoundly affect existence." Yet, by anyone not trained in the Marxian dialectic, the nature of the complexity is not hard to recognise. There seems no reason for repeating the argument of "*Under Which King, Bezonian?*" that the dialectic itself brings the Marxist to the point at which he must contemplate a quite different relation between culture and the economic process from that of the past. To put it simply, instead of dictating to the mass of mankind their uses of time, the economic process will free their time, in large measure, for uses dictated by inner human nature, if there should be one capable of dictating.

But is there such a thing as "inner human nature?" The Marxian theory (and historical forecast) would seem to leave little room for it, though implicitly postulating the need for a very potent one, to take over when the Class War ends and the economic process recedes into unobtrusiveness; and that is why the Marxian future looks so vacuous, Wellsian and bourgeois. That mechanical efficiency should be a religion for Russia, and ever more ambitious engineering a sufficient future, is, in the present phase, understandable and perhaps necessary. But, however badly civilisation may work, the West can imagine a "technocratic" or "planned economy" America too easily to find it an inspiring vision; a more adequate incitement to devoted activity is needed, and needed at once.

We assume an "inner human nature,"[1] and our recognition that it may be profoundly affected by the "economic process" persuades us that it must rally, gather its resources and start training itself for its ultimate responsibility at once. A cogent way in which the human spirit can refute the Marxian theory and the bourgeois negative lies open in education. "*L'éducation pourra tout*," the correspondent referred to above credits us with believing: that, perhaps, is answered. "*Scrutiny* will, no doubt, offer destructive analyses of education as it is—there are precedents enough—but the Scrutineers will effect no change." If we do not make the obvious and modest response, that is not because we rate our own powers or importance high, but because we know that we speak (having the luck to be in a position to do so) for a formidable and growing body of conviction. Whether or not

[1] Some readers, of course, will demand more at this point, appealing to "the judgments of the experience of the race."

we are "playing the capitalist game" should soon be apparent, for a serious effort in education involves the fostering of a critical attitude towards civilisation as it is. Perhaps there will be no great public outcry when it is proposed to introduce into schools a training in resistance to publicity and in criticism of newspapers—for this is the least opposable way of presenting the start in a real modern education. Yet the inevitable implications, accompaniments and consequences of such a training hardly need illustrating.

The teaching profession is peculiarly in a position to do revolutionary things; corporate spirit there can be unquestionably disinterested, and by a bold challenge there, perhaps the self-devotion of the intelligent may be more effectively enlisted than by an appeal to the Class War.

"THIS POETICAL RENASCENCE"

AMERICA, in Harriet Monroe's *Poetry*, has long had a magazine devoted to verse. Persistence over twenty years is in a way impressive, though just what it signifies is, perhaps, not easily summed up. *Poetry* quotes on its back cover from Whitman:

> To have great poets
> there must be great audiences too.

At any rate, if there were no audience at all we couldn't expect to have many poets, and, moreover, there would in any case be little point in having them. The intention, so admirably persisted in, that founded *Poetry* was that poets should be assured of an audience; and there can be no doubt that by printing the early work of poets who have since achieved distinction, *Poetry* did help them to develop. But it must be asked, in what sense is there to-day a public for verse? Is there more a public now than there was twenty years ago?

It will be well, not to be invidious, to turn at this point nearer home. *New Verse* is to be welcomed, and commended for support, as undertaking on this side of the Atlantic a like office to that of the American magazine. One is glad to read in the second number that "the first number of *New Verse* has sold well, and validates trust that both need and public for it exist." Nevertheless, it must be said, with reference to the questions just asked, that *New Verse* points to the same answer as *Poetry*. And, to be quite uninvidious, so does all the recent evidence that journalists speaking of the growing public for poetry would adduce. *Poetry*, *New Verse*, *New Signatures*, *New Country*, the *Hogarth Living Poets*, and one might add, to maintain the international balance, the verse pages of the *Symposium* and the *Hound and Horn*—journals specified because of their intelligence—all go to show that there is not in any serious sense a public for poetry. A real public for poetry would be a public in some degree educated about poetry, and capable of appreciating and checking critically the editorial standards; a public embodying a certain collective experience, intelligence and taste. The good editorial critic would be the representative of the highest level of such a public (most present to him, probably, in the form of an immediate milieu of critical exchange and discussion). Where there is no such public the critic is without the means to education he has a right to and without the necessary conditions of functioning. And if one says that the contents of the publications referred to make it impossible to believe that such a public exists, that is not to disparage insultingly those editorially responsible.

To make a start where everything has to be done from the beginning, to assemble the nucleus of an actively and intelligently responsive public, and to form in commerce with it the common critical sensibility that every individual critic assumes, and has to assume if he is to be a critic at all, is a desperately difficult business. It might be said that *New Verse*, *New Signatures* and the associated publications (for though *New Verse* is independent in editorship and intention it clearly depends upon the same general response as the others) do at any rate represent a notably determined and promising effort at a start. The reception they have had—there has been a general readiness to hail achievement, to see a new phase of English poetry as actually here—certainly evidences a fairly widely shared sense that to have a poetry that should be a significant part of contemporary life is desirable. Both this sense and the accompaning readiness are representatively expressed in Mr. Michael Roberts's prefaces to *New Signatures* and *New Country*. The complete discrepancy between the preface (richly illustrative of the procreant wish) and the following contents, between sales-talk and goods, make the earlier book, which came out last year, especially interesting.

It was, to begin with, a striking enough achievement to see any community among so heterogeneous an array of versifiers. But Mr. Roberts is capable, in offering his book as representing "a clear reaction against esoteric poetry in which it is necessary for the reader to catch each recondite allusion," of picking on Mr. Empson as exemplary, and finding his poems "important because they do something to remove the difficulties which have stood between the poet and the writing of popular poetry." Mr.

Empson, as a matter of fact, is at least as recondite and difficult here as he has ever been, and several of the poems leave one wondering whether the difficulty is worth wrestling with. The uneasiness that qualified the interest one took in Mr. Empson's work long before he became a New Signature is settling into sad recognition that he is becoming less and less likely to develop. He seems no nearer than before to finding a more radical incitement to the writing of poetry (or of criticism) than pleasure in a strenuous intellectual game. He is very intelligent indeed, but he is an odd recruit for the company of the devoted who, whatever they may lack as poets, at least have, or lay claim to, the qualification that I agree with Mr. Roberts in thinking essential if we are to hope for a "poetical renascence"—moral seriousness, or moral passion (for the tone of Mr. Roberts's prefaces comports with the stronger phrase).

"The technical achievement of these poets is notable" runs the preface to *New Signatures*: of Mr. Empson alone is it true. (Unless one excepts also Mr. Eberhart, an American poet who appears to be included merely because he figured in *Cambridge Poetry*, 1929. Though he is the antithesis of Mr. Empson in being a poet of naïve emotion and intuition, he will, because of his intensely individualist sensibility and expression, be found by most readers almost as obscure and "esoteric," and not even with the severest strain can one see him as belonging in a Communist or Public School context. As of

Mr. Empson's, though for opposite reasons, one has doubts about his development; but this is an opportunity to recall his remarkable long poem, *A Bravery of Earth*, which came out a year or two ago and deserves more attention than it got.) Of the others, those who are qualified by intention for the desiderated new poetic order are notably lacking in technical achievement, even when they give signs of talent—especially then, for it is where the talented are concerned that the point is significant: a lack of due development in them, a lack of that sureness of self-realisation, that awareness of essential purpose, which registers itself in technique, is just what one would expect in the absence of an intelligent public.

The absence of such a public is the most conclusive evidence of the absence of an effective contemporary sensibility, that general sensibility of an age to which the individual sensibility, whatever the conscious intention, is always related. A work of art, we can hardly remind ourselves too often, is never a merely individual achievement.

At any rate, the disadvantage of having no critical reception to expect is readily recognised. Neglect is not the only wrong an artist may suffer: uncritical acclamation may cheer him but it will hardly do him any good. And uncritical acclamation has been the misfortune of Mr. W. H. Auden in particular, the dominating force in the new movement (for there really is a movement). When his "Charade," *Paid on Both Sides*, appeared in the *Criterion* several years ago there was good reason to be impressed: here was an undoubted new talent of impressive potentialities. But why when his first book, *Poems*, containing the "Charade," appeared he should have been discerned at once by all the "discerning" (see the publishers' blurb on the dust-cover of *The Orators*) as a major luminary, and established in permanent acceptance, isn't easy to explain, for he is, while being neither nice nor like Mr. Richard Aldington, extremely difficult, and one can say with confidence that none of the critics who acclaimed him in superlative terms understood him or were irresistibly thrilled by him. But he is now well known to the *Listener* public and annotated marginally by dons.

Of *The Orators* its reviewer in our weightiest literary review, while finding it (no mere modesty, as he went on to show) "exceedingly difficult to understand, but in spite of this extraordinarily stimulating," had "no doubt that it is the most valuable contribution to English poetry since *The Waste Land*. The last ten years have been singularly unfruitful; the next ten years will show whether the promise in Mr. Auden's first volume of poems, published eighteen months ago, is fulfilled, as I believe it will be."—The promise was undoubtedly there, and if it is fulfilled it will be in spite of the general reception exemplified by this encouraging reviewer. Mr. Auden is a highly intelligent man, and probably has his own opinion of his acclaimers. But in his kind of undertaking, in which it is so difficult to draw the line between necessary and unnecessary obscurity, he was peculiarly in need of the check represented by intelligent criticism and the expectation of it.

Some of the obscurity of the *Poems* was certainly unjustified; the signs of insufficiently sharp and sure realisation were frequent; the notation was often both too general—a matter of vague gestures, and too personal—relying too much on private associations. But everyone knows now that modern poetry is difficult, that one doesn't expect to understand much, that one jumps from point to point, "excited" or "stimulated" by an image here and a rhythm there. Mr. Garman, reviewing *The Orators* in *Scrutiny* for September last, noted the significant use by the publishers of the word "obscure."

Anyway, *The Orators* (as Mr. Garman also noted) compared with *Poems* exhibits a falling-off. How distinguished a talent Mr. Auden can command the extraordinarily good opening piece in prose, *Address for a Prize-Day*, reminds us. But from the book as a whole it is plain that he has presumed on the reader's readiness to see subtlety and complexity in the undefined and unorganised, and has been too often content to set down what came more or less as it came. The adverse judgment, which might have remained longer suspended, is precipitated by an unignorable element of something like undergraduate cleverness, and where the level of seriousness is so uncertain, the benefit of the doubt—the doubt at any point where the effort demanded of the reader is worth making—hardly accrues to the author.

There is reason, then, to deplore the uncritical acclamation that Mr. Auden has had to suffer. But in his case extravagance was comparatively reasonable, his talent being impressive; and his talent being also robust, we may hope that it will develop in spite of all. But when Mr. Stephen Spender is treated in the same way it is hard to look on with any patience. The publishers, on the dust-cover, give the cue: "If Auden is the satirist of this poetical renascence, Spender is its lyric poet. In his work the experimentalism of the last two decades is beginning to find its reward. . . . Technically, these poems appear to make a definite step forward in English poetry."

Such a blurb as this from a firm with associations as distinguished as Messrs. Faber and Faber's is peculiarly lamentable (one remembers the one for Mr. Herbert Read, which announced that, though different, he was a poet as important as Mr. Eliot). Whoever was allowed to write it knew nothing about poetry—though that, perhaps, the public being what it is, was after all no serious disqualification. However that may be, the first thing anyone accustomed to reading poetry notices in Mr. Spender's verse is that though there are, perhaps, signs of a genuine impulse and a personal sensibility the technique is very immature and unstable. So far from being the subtle end-product of "the experimentalism of the last two decades," Mr. Spender is unformed enough to be able to reproduce (quite unwittingly, it seems) the Meredith of *Modern Love*:

> My parents quarrel in the neighbour room.
> "How did you sleep last night?" "I woke at four
> To hear the wind that sulks along the floor
> Blowing up dust like ashes from the tomb."
>
> "I was awake at three." "I heard the moth
> Breed perilous worms." "I wept
> All night, watching your rest." "I never slept
> Nor sleep at all." Thus ghastly they speak, both.

As for such pieces as the following, one would hardly talk about "technique," but of the underlying immaturity, the absence of any realised personal response, of any precise, consistent feeling or vision to communicate:

> Hopelessly wound round with the cords of street
> Men wander down their lines of level graves.
> Sometimes the maze knots into flaring caves
> Where magic lantern faces skew for greeting.
> Smile dawns with a harsh lightning, there's no speaking
> And, far from lapping laughter, all's parched and hard.
> Here the pale lily boys flaunt their bright lips,
> Such pretty cups for money, and older whores
> Skuttle rat-toothed into the dark outdoors.

The transition to the *Sinister Street* of the end of the passage is a comment on the realistic-sinister of the opening, where the imagery—"wound," "cords," "level graves," "maze," "knots" and so on—is quite unrealised; thought of from the outside, rather than felt in.

Slightly disguised in the technical modernising, there is a good deal of Georgian; the following, indeed, might have come from one of the anthologies:

> I hear the cries of evening, while the paw
> Of dark creeps up the turf;
> Sheep's bleating, swaying gull's cry, the rook's caw,
> The hammering surf.
>
> I am inconstant yet this constancy
> Of natural rest twangs at my heart;
> Town-bred, I feel the roots of each earth-cry
> Tear me apart.

Sincere? One does not doubt it; but "sincere" is not a very useful term in criticism. The glamorous-ineffable-vague to which Mr. Spender is given, and which, perhaps, accounts as much as anything for the emphasis on "lyric" in the blurb quoted above, is obviously sincere:

> Your body is stars whose million glitter here:
> I am lost amongst the branches of this sky
> Here near my breast, here in my nostrils, here
> Where our vast arms like streams of fire lie.
>
> How can this end? My healing fills the night
> And hangs its flags in worlds I cannot near.
> Our movements range through miles, and when we kiss
> The moment widens to enclose long years.

It may be "in a tradition which reaches back to the early Greek lyric poets" (the blurb again), but it has nothing in particular to do with the technical experimenting of the last two decades.

The official account, then, is preposterously unfair to Mr. Spender, and the contemporary cultural situation it reflects, peculiarly unfavourable to the development of such a talent as his. Favourable reviews and a reputation are no substitute for the conditions represented by the existence of an intelligent public—the give-and-take that is necessary for self-realisation, the pressure that, resisted or yielded to, determines direction, the intercourse that is collaboration (such collaboration as produces language, an analogy that, here as so often when art is in question, will repay a good deal of reflecting upon: the individual artist to-day is asked to do far too much for himself and far too much as an individual).

In the absence of these conditions it is natural to make the most of the Group:

> Wystan, Rex, all of you that have not fled,
> This is our world. . . .

writes Mr. Day Lewis. And it is difficult to see how a start can be made in any other way. But the very circumstances that make the Group essential enhance its disadvantages and dangers—some of them at any rate, even when the purpose is to work towards a new popular poetry:

> Lipcurl, Swiveleye, Bluster, Crock and Queer,
> Mister I'll-think-it-over, Miss Not-to-day,
> Young Who-the-hell-cares and old Let-us-pray,
> Sir Après-moi-le-déluge. It is here
> They get their orders. These will have to pay.

—For what public is this? It is certainly not esoteric; indeed, the simplicity is of a kind that one would have found appropriate in verse dedicated, as Mr. Auden dedicates some of his (not so simple), "To my pupils." As a little-language within the Group and its immediate connections such a mode no doubt has its uses, but in what spirit is it offered to the general public? Mr. Day Lewis employs it a great deal in *The Magnetic Mountain*, and what is more significant, mixes it with modes that belong to quite another plane—that can be considered as serious efforts towards the desiderated new poetry. One sees reflected in this uncertainty of purpose and level a confusion, very natural where the Group counts for so much and is the only certain audience, of the public occasion and context with the familiar. By any standards it is a curious instability that is exhibited here:

> Iron in the soul,
> Spirit steeled in fire,
> Needle trembling on truth—
> These shall draw me there.
>
> The planets keep their course,
> Blindly the bee comes home,
> And I shall need no sextant
> To prove I'm getting warm.
>
> Near that miraculous mountain
> Compass and clock must fail,
> For space stands on its head there
> And time chases its tail.

In the following, as often, there is a show of dramatic presentment, but this makes no apparent difference to the spirit in which the mode is offered:

> You'll be leaving us soon and it's up to you boys,
> Which shall it be? You must make your choice.
> There's a war on, you know. Will you take your
>   stand
> In obsolete forts or in no-man's land?

Even in Mr. Auden, in his simple and often admirable guerrilla vein, the irony sometimes slips into something dangerously close to this House-master-Kipling-Chesterton simplicity. It seems relevant to note at this point that both in *Paid on Both Sides* and in *The Orators* there is a Public School background (and, one might add, a romantic element, qualifying the remarkable maturity, and drawing, one guesses, on memories of a childhood spent during the War). Indeed, to those who are not Public School—and to others, too, no doubt—the Communism of the Group offers an interesting study. Mr. Auden contributed a *Song* to the first number of *New Verse*:

> I'll get a job in a factory
> I'll live with working boys
> I'll play them at darts in the public house
> I'll share their sorrows and joys
> Not live in a world that has had its day.
>
> They won't tell you their secrets
> Though you pay for their drinks at the bar
> They'll tell you lies for your money
> For they know you for what you are
> That you live in a world that has had its day.

Ah! those secrets—and that superiority—of the working boys. There are a number of other verses in this very interesting simple mode, and the whole forms a curious psychological document, the more curious because of the undoubted subtlety of Mr. Auden's mind. The Editor of *New Signatures* thinks that Communism may favour satire, but it certainly hasn't given Mr. Auden a secure basis yet.

This criticism is offered with the reverse of a malicious intention. That a group of young writers, uniting a passionate and responsible concern about the state of contemporary civilisation with a devotion to poetry, should have won some kind of public recognition is something. It would be a pity if a serious propagandist spirit should let itself get confused with a kind of higher boy-scouting, or the new poetic movement degenerate into a new Georgianism (Mrs. Naomi Mitchison's contribution in the communal style to the first number of *New Verse* would have been worth the printing if it served as a comic warning).

To this new Georgianism Mr. Roy Campbell would stand as the Flecker. True, he infuses Parnassian rotundity with Byronic energy (He taught us little: but our soul had *felt* him like the thunder's roll), but he stands decidedly for Form—Form as the classically trained recognise it. He recognises himself in *The Albatross* (*after Baudelaire*):

> Like him the shining poet sunward steers,
> Whose rushing plumes the hurricanes inflate,

and the mastery with which he rides his hurricanes is really impressive. It is a genuine talent, and the conviction with which it is used, at this date, remarkable. One reflects sadly of the movement towards a new popular poetry considered above that not even its nearest approximations will be widely read. Mr. Campbell's verse, lyrical or satiric, is much less remote from popularity, and it is probably read—and not merely bought—by what may be called, comparatively, a public.

It would not be surprising to learn that Mr. Aldington's is read by a much larger, for it is "free," "modernist" (as Mr. Harold Nicolson would say) and yet "as easy to read as a novel."

Mr. George Reavey's *Faust's Metamorphoses*, which is not naïve in its sophistication, has no public, and is the product of conditions in which no public for poetry exists. The cosmopolitan background of his introspections merely heightens or makes more obvious the common disabilities that the potential poet suffers to-day. To be so free to experiment in idiom and technique, to have so many possibilities before one—these are disadvantages that only remarkable genius could begin to overcome. It is as if the individual hadn't even a language to hand, but had to create one, and it is not only because of the problem of communication that an individually created language will be unsatisfactory.

The late Harry Crosby, an American living in France, actually uses a completely private language in some of his poems:

Sthhe fous on ssu eod
Ethueeu touud on ssu eod
Htetouethdu tds foett
Fhtdeueeue on ssu eod

A game? The volume from which this comes has an introduction by D. H. Lawrence. The other three volumes are introduced by T. S. Eliot, Ezra Pound and Stuart Gilbert. Lawrence's volume contains this:

"black black black black black
black black black black black
black black black black black
black black black black black
black black Sun black black
black black black black black
black black black black black
black black black black black
black black black black black"

Mr. Eliot, in his introduction, says he thinks we find, "in Crosby's writings, that we do not pick out single poems for enjoyment: if any of it is worth reading, then it all is." It should, however, be said that most of the pieces answer more ostensibly to Mr. Eliot's general account: "Harry Crosby's verse was consistently, I think, the result of an effort to record as exactly as possible to his own satisfaction a particular way of apprehending life." "What interests me most, I find," says Mr. Eliot later, "is his search for a personal symbolism of imagery." But one gathers that he means to disclaim any suggestion that he understands. Crosby's language, that is, remains predominately a private one.

Harry Crosby, it is plain, was a very charming person. The set of four slim, beautifully produced volumes,[1] so illustriously sponsored, looks like being one of the most interesting literary curiosities of the age.

1933.

[1] *Transit of Venus:* With a Preface by T. S. Eliot. *Torch-bearer:* With Notes by Ezra Pound. *Chariot of the Sun:* Introduction by D. H. Lawrence. *Sleeping Together:* With a Memory of the Poet by Stuart Gilbert.

JOYCE AND "THE REVOLUTION OF THE WORD"[1]

TO judge the *Work in Progress*, in any bulk, not worth the labour of reading is not necessarily to identify oneself with the late Poet Laureate. One may find some of the propositions with which the hierophants of the Mystic Logos seek to stagger the world commonplace—one may think Gerard Manley Hopkins the greatest poet of the Victorian Age—and yet regret the use to which James Joyce has put his genius since he finished *Ulysses*. There is no question of appealing to even the Oxford English Dictionary or even the most modern English Grammar as authorities. "In developing his medium to the fullest, Mr. Joyce is after all doing only what Shakespeare has done in his later plays, such as *The Winter's Tale* and *Cymbeline*, where the play-wright obviously embarked on new word sensations before reaching that haven of peacefulness," etc.—in demurring to such a proposition, and replying that Mr. Joyce is, after all, not doing only what Shakespeare has done, one's

[1] *Transition*, I–VIII, XI–XIII, XV, XVIII and XXII. *Anna Livia Plurabelle*, James Joyce. *Haveth Childers Everywhere*, James Joyce. *Two Tales of Shem and Shaun*, James Joyce. *Our Exagmination Round his Factification for Incamination of Work in Progress*, Samuel Beckett and others: Shakespeare & Co., 1929. *The Language of Night* (Transition Series, No. 1), Eugene Jolas.

objection is not that he takes particular licences unprecedented in the plays.

Mr. Joyce's liberties with English are essentially unlike Shakespeare's. Shakespeare's were not the product of a desire to "develop his medium to the fullest," but of a pressure of something to be conveyed. One insists, it can hardly be insisted too much, that the study of a Shakespeare play must start with the words; but it was not there that Shakespeare—the great Shakespeare—started: the words matter because they lead down to what they came from. He was in the early wanton period, it is true, an amateur of verbal fancies and ingenuities, but in the mature plays, and especially in the late plays stressed above, it is the burden to be delivered, the precise and urgent command from within, that determines expression—tyrannically. That is Shakespeare's greatness: the complete subjection—subjugation—of the medium to the uncompromising, complex and delicate need that uses it. Those miraculous intricacies of expression could have come only to one whose medium was for him strictly a medium; an object of interest only as something that, under the creative compulsion, identified itself with what insisted on being expressed: the linguistic audacities are derivative.

Joyce's development has been the other way. There is prose in *Ulysses*, the description, for instance, of Stephen Dedalus walking over the beach, of a Shakespearian concreteness; the rich complexity it offers to analysis derives from the intensely imagined experience realised in the words. But in the *Work in Progress*, it is plain, the interest in words and their possibilities comes first. The expositors speak of "Mr. Joyce's linguistic experiments"; and: "That he is following the most modern philological researches can be deduced from the passage . . ." (*Transition* XXII, p. 103). We are explicitly told that "words evoke in him more intense emotions than the phenomena of the outer world" (*Exagmination*, etc., p. 153). Mustering his resources, linguistic and philological, (and, one hears, with the aid of an Interpreting Bureau), he stratifies his puns deeper and deeper, multiplies his associations and suggestions, and goes over and over his text, enriching and complicating.

"Few authors ever wrote a sentence with a more complete consciousness of every effect they wished to obtain" (*Exagmination*, etc., p. 67)—but the wished effect (it would be self-evident, even without the successive versions extant of given passages) develops continually at the suggestion of the words; more and more possibilities of stratification and complication propose themselves. Working in this way, "inserting his new ideas continually in whatever part of the supple text they are appropriate" (*Exagmination*, etc., p. 164), Mr. Joyce achieves complexities that offer themselves as comparable to Shakespeare's. But, achieved in this way, they betray at once their essential unlikeness. "The obscurity of that passage, its prolixity and redundancy, all are deliberately and artistically logical"

(*Exagmination*, etc., p. 55). Nothing could be "righter" than Shakespeare's effects, but they are irreconcilable with this kind of deliberate, calculating contrivance and with this external approach. They register the compulsive intensity and completeness with which Shakespeare realises his imagined world, the swift immediacy that engages at a point an inexhaustibly subtle organisation.

The contrast would still have held even if Shakespeare had had (as we are convinced he had not) to achieve his organisation by prolonged and laborious experiment, and his immediacy with corresponding critical toil. The essential is that the words are servants of an inner impulse or principle of order; they are imperiously commanded and controlled from an "inner centre."

In the *Work in Progress*, even in the best parts, we can never be unaware that the organisation is external and mechanical. Each line is a series of jerks, as the focus jumps from point to point; for the kind of attention demanded by each one of the closely packed "effects" is incompatible with an inclusive, co-ordinating apprehension. The kind of accent and intonation with which a pun announces itself refuse to be suppressed; they are persistent and devastating. Many of the effects are undoubtedly interesting; *Anna Livia Plurabelle* is in some ways a very striking—and, rendered by Joyce himself, one can believe, a pleasing—performance. But in anything resembling an integrated effect a very large part indeed of the intended complexity must be lost: "It is possibly necessary to 'trance' oneself into a state of word-intoxication, flitting concept-inebriation," says one of the expositors (*Exagmination*, etc., p. 114). The "meaning," or an impressive amount of it, can always be worked out at leisure, just as it was worked in (the opportunities that the *Work in Progress* offers for knowing elucidation insure it a certain popularity; it is surprising, Paris having long enough ago given the cue, that our undergraduate intellect stays content with the *Cantos*). But, at the best, the satisfaction provided even by *Anna Livia Plurabelle* is incommensurate with the implicit pretensions and with the machinery. It is significant that, for the English-speaking reader, so much of the satisfaction remains in the French translation published (with an amusing account of the method of translating) in the *Nouvelle Revue Française* (1931, vol. xxxvi, p. 633).

To justify a medium much less obtrusive in pretensions than that of the *Work in Progress* Joyce would have had to have a commanding theme, animated by some impulsion from the inner life capable of maintaining a high pressure. Actually the development of the medium appears to be correlated with the absence of such a theme—to be its consequence. For in the earlier work, in *Ulysses* and before, the substance is clearly the author's personal history and the pressure immediately personal urgency; the historical particularity is explicit enough and it is hardly impertinent to say that *Ulysses* is clearly a catharsis. But if one asks what controls the interest in technique, the preoccupation with the means of expression, in the *Work in Progress*, the answer is a reference to Vico; that is, to a philosophical theory.

"Vico proposed the making of 'an ideal and timeless history in which all the actual histories of all nations should be embodied.'" (*Exagmination* etc., p. 51.) He also contemplated the formation of a "mental vocabulary" "whose object should be to explain all languages that exist by an ideal synthesis of their varied expressions. And now, after two centuries, such a synthesis of history and language, a task which seemed almost beyond human achievement, is being realised by James Joyce in his latest work" (*Exagmination*, etc., p. 54). A certain vicious bent manifested itself very disturbingly in *Ulysses*, in the inorganic elaborations and pedantries and the evident admiring belief of the author in Stephen's intellectual distinction, and the idea of putting Vico's theory of history into the concrete would seem rather to derive from this bent than to be calculated to control it.

In any case the idea would seem to be self-stultifying. The result in the *Work in Progress* of trying to put "allspace in a notshall"—the "ideal" (but concrete) "and timeless history" in a verbal medium defying all linguistic conventions—is not orchestrated richness but, for the most part, monotonous non-significance. Forms, after all, in life and art, are particular and limiting, and *The Waste Land* probably goes about as far as can be gone in the way of reconciling concrete particularity with inclusive generality. Joyce's limitless ambition leads to formlessness, local and in survey. The "ideal history" would seem to be chaos, that which precedes form—or swallows it. In it, "movement is non-directional—or multi-directional, and a step forward is, by definition, a step back" (*Exagmination,* etc., p. 22). H.C.E. (Humphrey Chimpden Earwicker) is glossed by "Here Comes Everybody"; but a multi-directional flux, though it may be said to have something like universality, has not the universality of a mythical figure. Joyce's medium, likewise, is not in the end rich. It may be the "esperanto of the subconscious"; if so, the subconscious is sadly boring.

As a matter of fact, Joyce's subconscious is worse than boring; it is offensively spurious. It is not that one objects to conscious management, which is inevitable. But conscious management in the *Work in Progress* is not the agent of a deeply serious purpose; it serves in general an inveterate solemn ingenuity, and it is often the very willing pimp to a poor wit. "Cosmic humour" there may be, as the expositors allege, in the *Work in Progress*: there is certainly a great deal of provocation for D. H. Lawrence's reaction: "My God, what a clumsy *olla putrida* James Joyce is! Nothing but old fags and cabbage-stumps of quotations from the Bible and the rest, stewed in the juice of deliberate, journalistic dirty-mindedness—what old and hard-worked staleness, masquerading as the all-new!"

There is more in the *Work in Progress* than that, but the spuriousness, the mechanical manipulation, is pervasive.

Lawrence, of course, objected to the whole thing; and his objection finds endorsement in the company Joyce keeps. It was fair to use the bits from his expositors quoted above, since it is not because he can get published nowhere else that he continues to appear in *Transition* : he, at any rate tacitly, encourages them. We are free to assume that the "International Workshop for Orphic Creation" (as *Transition* now describes itself) is under his patronage, and that he does not dissociate himself from his expositors when they issue manifestoes in favour of "The Vertigral Age":

> "The Vertigral Age believes that we stand in direct line with the primeval strata of life.
>
> * * * * *
>
> The Vertigral Age wants to give voice to the ineffable silence of the heart.
>
> The Vertigral Age wants to create a primitive grammar, the stammering that approaches the language of God."

Joyce (who gives "such a picture of the entire universe as might be registered in the mind of some capricious god") is said to have "desophisticated language" ("Vico applied to the problem of style"). It is, on the contrary, plain that the whole phenomenon is one of sophistication, cosmopolitan if not very subtle, and, so far from promising a revival of cultural health, is (it does not need Lawrence's nostril to detect) a characteristic symptom of dissolution. The "internationalisation of language" acclaimed by Joyce's apostles is a complementary phenomenon to Basic English; indeed, we note with a surprised and pleased sense of fitness that Mr. C. K. Ogden has shown an active interest in the *Work in Progress*.

Their conception of the problem—"I claim for *transition*," says Mr. Eugene Jolas, "priority in formulating the problem on an international scope . . . and in giving it a dialectical substructure"—is ludicrously inadequate. "I believe," says Mr. Jolas, standing up for the artist, "in his right to audaciously split the infinitive." As if any amount of splitting infinitives, mimicking the Master, pondering Gertrude Stein and E. E. Cummings and connoisseuring American slang, could revivify the English language.

A brief reflection on the conditions of Shakespeare's greatness is in place here. He represents, of course, the power of the Renaissance. But the power of the Renaissance could never so have manifested itself in English if English had not already been there—a language vigorous enough to respond to the new influx, ferment and literary efflorescence, and, in so doing, not lose, but strengthen its essential character. The dependence of the theatre on both Court and populace ensured that Shakespeare should use his "linguistic genius"[1]

[1] " . . . considering how few other writers have added idioms to the language, it is a surprising proof, both of his linguistic genuis and his popularity . . ." Logan Pearsall Smith, *Words and Idioms*, p. 229. (The context—and, indeed, a great part of the essay—bears peculiarly upon the question under discussion.)

—he incarnated the genius of the language—to the utmost. And what this position of advantage represents in a particular form is the general advantage he enjoyed in belonging to a genuinely national culture, to a community in which it was possible for the theatre to appeal to the cultivated and the populace at the same time.

A national culture rooted in the soil—the commonplace metaphor is too apt to be rejected: the popular basis of culture was agricultural. Mr. Logan Pearsall Smith shows how much of the strength and subtlety of English idiom derives from an agricultural way of life. The essential nature of the debt is well suggested by his notes on phrasal verbs. "For when we examine these phrasal verbs, we find that by far the greater number of them also render their meanings into terms of bodily sensation. They are formed from simple verbs which express the acts, notions, and attitudes of the body and its members; and these, combining with prepositions like 'up,' 'down,' 'over,' 'off,' etc. (which also express ideas of motion), have acquired in addition to their literal meanings, an enormous number of idiomatic significations, by means of which the relations of things to each other, and a great variety of the actions, feelings and thoughts involved in human intercourse, are translated, not into visual images, but into what psychologists call 'kinæsthetic' images, that is to say, sensations of the muscular efforts which accompany the attitudes and motions of the body." (*Words and Idioms*, p. 250.)

This strength of English belongs to the very spirit of the language—the spirit that was formed when the English people who formed it was predominantly rural. Why it should be associated with a rural order, why it should develop its various resources to the fullest there, Mr. Adrian Bell, illustrating the vigour and fineness of rustic speech in the last number of *Scrutiny*,[1] suggested: he showed "how closely the countryman's life and language grow together; they are like flesh and bone." They grow together just as mind and body, mental and physical life, have grown together in those phrasal verbs. And how much richer the *life* was in the old, predominantly rural order than in the modern suburban world one must go to the now oft-cited George Bourne (under both his names) for an adequate intimation. When one adds that speech in the old order was a popularly cultivated art, that people talked (so making Shakespeare possible) instead of reading or listening to the wireless, it becomes plain that the promise of regeneration by American slang, popular city-idiom or the inventions of transition-cosmopolitans is a flimsy consolation for our loss.

It is an *order* that is gone—Mr. Bell records its last remnants—and there are no signs of its replacement by another: the possibility of one that should offer a like richness of life, of emotional, mental and bodily life in association, is hardly even imaginable. Instead we have cultural disintegration,

[1] June 1933.

mechanical organisation and constant rapid change. There seems no time for anything to grow, even if it would. If the English people had always been what they are now there would have been no Shakespeare's English and no comparable instrument: its life and vigour are no mere matter of vivid idioms to be matched by specimens of American slang (English, it may be ventured, has been more alive in America in the last century than in England mainly because of pioneering conditions, which are as unlike those of the modern city as possible).

At any rate, we still have Shakespeare's English: there is indeed reason in setting great store by the "word"—if not in the revolutionary hopes of Mr. Jolas and his friends. With resources of expression that would not have existed if Shakespeare's England had not been very different from his own, Gerard Manley Hopkins wrote major poetry in the Victorian Age. We have poets in our own day, and James Joyce wrote *Ulysses*. For how long a cultural tradition can be perpetuated in this way one wonders with painful tension. Language, kept alive and rejuvenated by literature, is certainly an essential means of continuity and transition—to what? We are back at the question, which has been raised in *Scrutiny* before and will be again, if *Scrutiny* performs its function, whether there can be a culture based on leisure, and if so, what kind.

We can demand no more than the certitude that

there are certain things to be done and cared for now. The line of reflection indicated above leads one to the unanswerable questions raised innocently by scientists who (in romantic or journalistic moments) speculate as to the complete transformation, physical and psychological, that Science will effect in Man.

1933.